Once a Cop, Always a Cop

Why Me?

LAWRENCE LAROSE

BALBOA
PRESS
A DIVISION OF HAY HOUSE

Balboa Press books may be ordered through booksellers or by contacting:

Balboa Press
A Division of Hay House
1663 Liberty Drive
Bloomington, IN 47403
www.balboapress.com
1 (877) 407-4847

Because of the dynamic nature of the Internet, any web addresses or links contained in this book may have changed since publication and may no longer be valid. The views expressed in this work are solely those of the author and do not necessarily reflect the views of the publisher, and the publisher hereby disclaims any responsibility for them.

The author of this book does not dispense medical advice or prescribe the use of any technique as a form of treatment for physical, emotional, or medical problems without the advice of a physician, either directly or indirectly. The intent of the author is only to offer information of a general nature to help you in your quest for emotional and spiritual well-being. In the event you use any of the information in this book for yourself, which is your constitutional right, the author and the publisher assume no responsibility for your actions.

Any people depicted in stock imagery provided by Thinkstock are models, and such images are being used for illustrative purposes only.
Certain stock imagery © Thinkstock.

Printed in the United States of America.

ISBN: 978-1-4525-9127-8 (sc)
ISBN: 978-1-4525-9128-5 (e)

Balboa Press rev. date: 3/14/2014

Acknowledgements

First and foremost, I would like to thank the Almighty God for His spiritual Guidance in my life. For this Autobiography would not have been possible. Also, I am very appreciative to the librarians at Rosedale and Rochdale Village Libraries for their invaluable support. I gave thanks to the staff, in the computer room at the New York City Parks Department at College Point, Flushing Queens NY. Last but not least, I thank Aaron and Alexis for the skillful Graphics that they have done, in order in getting my thoughts and concepts over to the readers.

Prologue

The purpose in writing this dramatic and exciting autobiography titled "**Once a Cop, Always a Cop**" is in providing the many readers, *that one's mind is the best weapon and the third eye, in surviving in this world.* What I am expressing is understood in not things too wonderful for me, which I knew not, but in my latter days, I am receiving spiritual guidance from God Himself, in having shown many visions on future events. I had some reservation and was very reluctant in writing this autobiography. But after reconsidering - it was not so difficult being unequivocal in reminiscing my past. I actually started digging deep down into my memory bank from a young age to date. It was like reincarnating in the reverse mode, going back to the many places and the people that I once knew.

This autobiography chronicles my life from childhood years in my native land of Guyana, South America. It continues with a momentous career in my country homeland's Police Academy, military and National Service; and having spent half of my adult life in such well known locations as New York's Wall Street; and in the Bronx, handling community affairs. My biography is based on the good, bad and ugly things that I had done during my journey in becoming an adult. Even though I consider myself a secretive and private person; I have no other choice in telling my life story to the readers, but some things are better left unsaid.

The chapters give detailed glimpses into my life during several important periods.

The memoire adds humor, found in stories and personal insight into many aspects of the book: Primarily, in keeping the mood light during more of the serious turns of the book. The headings of some chapters will not coincide with the episodes in the book. My memoire will trigger the minds of readers or visionaries of the future generation, in accomplishing whatsoever they set their minds, goals and objectives in accomplishing In the section capturing the visions sent to me by God is thoroughly enlightening, as to how accurate the visions are, in comparison to the actual events. Regarding those visions is quite exceptional. They depict more of a growing relationship with the Creator of all things in this world.

Once a Cop, Always a Cop is an engaging, but thought – provoking account of my life, and how in surrendering my entire being to the Almighty God. It changed my mindset towards the future, especially with the God given visions. I have acquired quite an extensive span of life experiences - viewed with a lighthearted spirit and appreciation from the life lessons gained. I have shattered the glass ceiling by establishing plans of action, which were timely, realistic and positive without adding a college degree to my name. But I did capitalize and never letting an opportunity passes me by. For being a solid achiever, it produced a tangible, but positive impact in my life through high performances in going above and beyond. "It's not where you come from it's where you're going".

Once a Cop, Always a Cop highlights the awareness what goes on in the big cities. However, a few police officers may have the ability in discerning what danger lies ahead. The lesson to learn as a parent is that you cannot bury your head in the sand, or ignoring the wrongs of your child. Many parents have lost their children to the world of evil – doers. However, in my growing up, I do appreciate my mother's continuous discipline, coupled with her epistle. It has made me live a longer life, and made me who I am today. I have maintained a mature attitude and a strong self control, in handling disappointments or inconsequential matters in my adult life. I had the slightest idea in what the future would bring and what the outcome will be. But at this point in my life, I know for a fact that the hands of God are resting on my shoulders. He has a big plan and task for me in carrying out; in accomplishing his task before my worldly flesh expires.

In writing my memoire, I was astounded, in knowing how much the brain is able to store in its cells and with so many episodes in my past. Some dramatic events that took place were temporary erased from my memory bank, (i.e. the time period covering from two years old to an age that I viewed and understood things). It also reminds me about dreaming, in coming to the great land of the United States of America and becoming a solid citizen.

While in my country of Guyana South America, both parents were overseas in the USA working very hard, in supporting their nine children back home. My mom had shipped a view master to me as a Christmas gift - a present that I cherished and joyfully looked at during the day and night. On these film slides, I viewed many tall buildings, wide roads and fancy motor cars, one nation of different races, color and beautiful parks. It was viewed in 3D and appearing almost real: Only in reaching out and touching that great, but a free land of America.

My Family Roots

My family heritage was Christian, but at such a young age, I had so much to learn in exactly where our previous generation had derived from. It is essential for me in mentioning my parents and one of my grandmothers. They all played an important role in my life. And before the existence of my generation, my mother got married to my father, who at that time was a teacher, before becoming a police officer. My mother was the only child for her mother and she lived alone with my grandmother in the suburbs. I was not quite acquainted with my mother side of the family. But, I later learned that one of her cousins was a doctor that managed his own private practice. My father side of the family was educators. His sister was a head teacher at a school and also his closest cousin. Other relatives residing in the USA are doctors.

My parents maintained nine children – five boys and four girls. My father died when I was in high school. My mother, who is currently ninety five years old and very healthy, is currently in a Nursing Home. Every visit I made to the nursing home – her monologue was *"God is my physician, and He alone is taking care of me"*. She still is having her wittiness and a great sense of humor. She almost raised me single handedly, and with both my parents coming from a humble origin.

In putting together the puzzles in my life, they kept me alive with the help of the Almighty God. Only at my adult age, I realized that the higher power has something in store for me in heaven and in the new world to come. Now, I have the task in completing my mission on this planet, in telling the truth to the readers about His creation and His plans for the future of humanity. (i.e. in reading my first book titled **"You are younger than your age"**. It will be giving you more in details about the future of man and mankind on this planet: Who is who, an accurate age of the world, a new compass and a new calendar that will be giving you your true age.

My biological father name is La Rose – a French surname *La Rose,* meaning the rose and belonging to a category of names as Rose that derived from a place in Jerusalem - a Hebrew name that resides in the land of Israel. Also, there is an alley in the city of Jerusalem which bores that name; and Christ carried His cross through that alleyway. The La Roses occupations in Israel and France were mainly horticulturists. They were high ranking military officers in the Grenadines during the eighteenth century. The first rose appeared in the city of Bethlehem as a result of prayers from a fair maiden. However, many of the La Rose's names can now be found in Haiti and Guyana, South America. That is, after expatriating to the Caribbean from the continent of Africa during the slave trade.

Before turning twelve years old, my life was in the hands of God and also with the full responsibilities of my parents. I was born in British Guiana a small country in South America; a land with vast jungle and three main rivers that are bordering the country – they are the Esequibo, Demerara and Berbice. My country is bordered by Brazil, Venezuela and Suriname with the vast gray Atlantic Ocean in the south. The name British Guiana was then one of the British colonies before gaining independence in 1967. It is an English speaking country: A nation composed of mainly East Indians and African descents. The native people are indigenous Amerindians from the Arawak and Carib tribes that lived along the Esequibo, Demerara and Berbice rivers. The population in the seventies was approximately 600,000 – 700,000 people of various cultures including the Chinese. Presently, the Chinese population is on the increase, and they're assisting in the development of the country in opening up many businesses. And the Portuguese are made up of a small percentage in the population.

The religions observed by the Indians were Hinduism and the Muslim faith. The blacks are from Africa and the Portuguese were mainly Christians; or they were converted to Christianity by British Missionaries. My father was very dedicated in the home. And I have adapted his way in doing grocery shopping in bulk, in having it lasting throughout the month, instead of grocery shopping on a weekly basis. My father's monthly salary in those days was about one hundred dollars. The cost of living was very low at that time - one affording to purchasing sugar at seven cents a pound.

My dad passed away while working on the job in the interior location in Guyana. Prior to that, he was promoted to a police inspector in the Auxiliary section of the police force. My mom became the sole bread - winner of the family. I went to his funeral at the church and parlor, but I did not eulogize. I did not know what the word eulogy had meant at the age of seventeen years old. What I can say now is that my father had good personal qualities: He was very pleasant; always relaxing in his favorite chair and smoking a cigarette. He had a strong moral character; he drank socially and he had displayed impeccable honesty. He was reliable and committed in putting food on our table. He was lacking the knowledge and skills in parental guidance to his nine kids. This is only my opinion; and it may not be the opinion of my other siblings.

I got married at a registrar office – riding on a bicycle and towing my bride to be in signing my life commitment and the responsibilities that followed. However, I had two girls with my wife, but I got a divorce. During my marriage, I had attended a church convention in Guyana. It was given by one Pastor Jones – not the infamous Pastor Jim Jones that killed over eight hundred people, by shooting and giving them poisonous cool aid to drink. Pastor Jones was giving a sermon in the church when he pointed me out, while I was standing way back, in a crowded church with the other believers. He beckoned me in coming forward in joining him on the stage, but I reluctantly went up feeling very humiliated. Then he rested his hand on my head saying, *"You are chosen by the Almighty God to be a great person."* He started speaking in tongues, along with some attendees in the church. It was my first

3

encounter having a Pastor prophesying to me; and it was witnessed by many people in the congregation.

As a kid growing up in my neighborhood and among many other kids around my age group, we were very mischievous in doing lots of tom – fooleries, and being competitive against each other in the streets. In our idle times we would take a dollar note - tying a thin long black thread to it, and then go hiding in tall bushes out of sight. The dollar bill was left lying in the middle of the road, but visible enough so that when someone is passing by they will recognize the money. As soon as they were bending down in picking it up, I would pull on the thread by moving the money towards me. They will then continue in attempting in grabbing at the money, but to no avail. After realizing it was a dirty trick that I was playing on them, they will usually leave and feeling very humiliated.

I joined a cub pack through the Catholic Church. The training groomed me into becoming self sufficient, self confidence and working together with other cubs in a team effort. The training also helped me in demonstrating an imaginative leadership qualities and competence, (i.e. when facing adversities in the field). After attaining an age in becoming a scout, I enrolled in one of the troops for a few months and left. The scout motto was "Be Prepared."- It has stuck in my head to this day.

Prior to 2002, I was trying very hard, in fulfilling my needs through my physical emotions and not the spiritual experiences in my day to day life. Presently, I have found hope, joy and lots of good in myself. I am sincerely working fervently only on the positive side of things. A sudden spiritual awakening has bestowed upon me from a higher p. I don't need anyone's spiritual advice or approval in staying free from sin. I am very comfortable in speaking my innermost feelings and my thoughts, in a supplication to the Almighty on a daily basis. He is my rock and best friend in whom I can trust one hundred percent. *Happy is the man who gains understanding, maintain sound wisdom and common sense.* In order in comprehending and effectively following the true sense in my book with God's systematic and unique method in him creating – it is by reading my book titled "**You are younger than your age**".

A Bold Move

My Genesis began at an early age and moving in my first home, in not such good neighborhood as I can vividly recall. It had two bedrooms with zero flushing toilets. The family utilized a latrine which was situated down wind in the back yard. It was approximately fifty feet on a board walk from the house in getting to the latrine. If I did not hate anything else in life – it was going into the latrine and smelling that stench on a daily basis. The bed pan was convenient to me, but I only used it at nights. Who would leave the house after midnight to be going through the dark with a flash light on a rainy night with thunder and lightening in using a latrine? There was an East Indian man who made the bridge over the trench his latrine. Every religious morning, he was seen stooping down on the bridge close to the water and easing him off in the trench. When the man finishes, he will use news paper in wiping himself off. At times, he was seen using a calabash with some water in bathing his buttocks.

I am the third boy and the fourth in a family of nine. Clothes were never a problem to me in my childhood days – hand me down was traditional. Mom was a self taught seamstress - altering my father's police trousers and giving the boys to wear at school, or wearing them for recreational purposes. My sisters were luckier in wearing skirts or dresses that were purchased from city stores. Flat iron was a popular item in those days – it was heated up on the stove and taken off in mom's perfect timing. Once I did tried using the flat iron on my favorite shirt, but the iron left a burnt imprint on the shirt and it also burnt my hand. The pots, pans and curling combs were made out of solid cast iron. Kerosene stove was used in the home before they were upgraded to propane gas – that is, only when we had moved to our new home. The house had no modern electricity, but only kerosene lanterns in providing not so bright light. My mother would move the lanterns from one room to another conveniently at night.

As a kid, hunting for candle flies in the dark night was my hubby. I placed a few of candle flies in a transparent bottle, in supplementing the light of the kerosene lamp. My brothers and sisters took baths, in using a bucket of water and a calabash for dipping out the water. Calabash is a large fruit deriving from a tree in tropical countries. The inside of the calabash is not good for human consumption. The salt soap was a multi – purpose soap and it was used for washing clothes, dishes and the floor or rubbing it on your body in taking a bath. And the carbolic antiseptic soap was used in the curing of soars on my skin. Our old home had an overhead wooden water reservoir on the outside at the left corner of the house. The reservoir provided drinking water to the kitchen and bathroom. When there is a down pouring of rain or storm, I would go outside butt naked and played in the rain – not fearing the thunder or the flashing of lightening.

My mom is a person with firm principles; but at times she would be flexible enough in bending the rules when I became older and increasingly becoming a more responsible teenager. I was ecstatic when learning that my parents had purchased a new home, which was approximately two miles away from our previous house. One day, at the age of five years old when both parents had left the house to go cleaning and preparing the new house, I bravely left home to go visiting the new house - knowingly when getting there my parents would be angry with me. First, I crossed a twenty feet canal walking through a cemetery, skipping from one grave unto another and then crossing another canal, before arriving at my destination. When my parents saw me, they were more surprised than becoming angry with me. To my expectation, the yard space was about fifty feet by forty feet. The ground floor consists of a small patio, kitchen, dining room and a living room. The upper floor contained three bedrooms, a flushing toilet and a bathroom - unlike the other house with the latrine in the back yard.

Exodus

At the age of nine years old, I recalled walking on my toe and ceased in doing so at the age of thirteen years old. I learned to ride a bicycle on my own accord, because it was a requirement, in getting a job at the grocery store in my immediate neighborhood. It did not take me any particular time, in learning to balance myself on a bicycle. But the Chinese grocery store had their own bicycle that carried a basket to the front of their bicycle so as to be fetching groceries. Normally the weight proportion was more to the front of the bike.

One day after loading the basket with groceries, in route to delivered at one of the resident's home. The back wheel of the bicycle lifted upwards when I pulled on the front brakes - spilling all items on the road and smashing bottles of Coco – Cola soda drinks. A matter of fact I was actually lighter in weight than the groceries in front of the bicycle. However, I quit that job in finding another summer holiday job; in weeding tall grass and bushes in the compound of businesses.

The exodus with the La Rosie bunch began when the family finally moved into our new house. The girls were given the first bedroom; my parents occupying the middle and the five boys had taken the last room. We all slept on the floor, using beddings as our buffer, except for our parents who had brought their bed over from the old house. Eventually, my dad bought new beds for the rest of us. The boys slept on double bunk beds with springs and coconut fiber mattresses with pillows that harbored bed bugs. Popping the bed bugs were much fun – the smell was unique from popping the lady - bugs.

I was frustrated with our living conditions, and I had respectfully questioned my mom why she brought forth so many children year after year apart. In placing us in a straight line, we looked like the steps outside our old house. But, I always respected and loved my mom dearly until this day. She was a disciplinarian, a good home maker and a small time farmer. In other words, she was able in doing anything possible under the sun, and in making the family comfortable. Her kitchen garden in front of the house had nine beds. Those beds resembled nine mud graves; with them having drains in between each bed, but they were flourishing with green vegetables of various kind.

The word tooth brush and tooth paste was not in my vocabulary, nor were those modern hygienic items available to us. We were taught in cutting a piece of limb off a black sage tree, five inches in length and peeling off its bark in cleaning our teeth. Cooking salt was used in place of tooth paste, and my tongue scraping was done with a knife. On a weekends once a month, my mom would dose us off with laxative – either drinking diluted Epsom salt, liquid cascara, castor oil or a Karela bitter bush with honey, so as to cut the bitter taste in my mouth. I cannot recall that anyone in the family ever got sick with influenza or with any other serious ailments. If that had taken place, the entire family would have been immobilized, because we were all clustered up in a small house.

When some of us in the family got constipated, my mom would apply warm water by inducing a rubber tube into our anuses and flushing out the waste matters. It was not painful, but it achieved it goal, in relieving one from the burden of the constipation.

Both grandparents had moved into our new home in a space of six months apart. My mom's mother was my favorite and cute looking grandmother who was about four feet ten inches short. One day, she took me fishing along a canal at a long distance away from our home. We had used earthworms for baiting the fishes, along with a strong rod that we normally cut from a special tree, and using nylon twine with a fish hook. My first catch was pulling up a long black eel. Never again did I go fishing with her, but instead, I assisted her in selling sugar cakes outside the Catholic school that I attended.

My grandparents moved into our new home, and they both died in the house within a few years apart. When both grandparents had separately passed away in our home, I witnessed as a kid two men arriving from the morgue, lifting the body off the bed and then dropping their bodies like a log unto a body bag that was spread out on the floor. For that sad moment of grief I was very angry, witnessing the way the dead was being disrespected and mishandled. I wanted to say something bad to those men, but I was cautious in doing so, because I was thought by my mom in respecting my elders.

A New Neighborhood

My constant assertiveness had made me unpopular among my brothers, coupled with my aggressive attitude and stubbornness. We frequently get into arguments and to the extent in threatening each other in a fist fight – but soon after we would maintain our brotherly love for each other. At the age of thirteen years old, my mom allowed me in returning home off the streets by midnight. At times, mom will be sleeping when I enter the house after 2:00 am in the morning.

There were lots of mosquitoes in the neighborhood. This was due to the stagnated waters in the drains and high grasses in alleyways. The mosquitoes usually spread malaria or filarial diseases in our country. The Health Ministry Department frequently dispatches one of their personnel in spraying DDT, a chemical that kills mosquitoes in the drains, stagnated waters and the high grasses. At nights, we burned mosquito coil repellants in the main rooms of the house, and supplementing that with mosquito nets. Sometime the mosquitoes will forcefully penetrated under the nets. But I became immune to their bites- or they had had enough of my boring blood.

At Christmas holidays, my mom would buy new drapes, new table cloth that was matching the drapes and floor linoleum. I always assisted her with the installation of the drapes; helping her in rolling out and spreading the linoleum on the floor.

We had cared for our pet dog named Rex. He was always getting into fights with other dogs, but appearing in getting the worst of it in the end – always returning limping and bleeding at the neck. In our immediate neighborhood, it was considered decent; but across the playing field and canal they were range houses called Laing Avenue. Frequent squabbles, profanities and fighting were taking place in their hallway. And at one time two brothers got into an altercation, which resulted into a fight while they were gambling for nickels and dimes. The younger brother claimed that he was cheated out of money by his older brother. So, the younger one took a machete and severing his brother's right hand from his body – only for twenty five cents. However, in the long run he was not sent to jail for that hideous crime that he had committed.

The jail house in Guyana during my teenage days was small for the population in the country. Most murderers were placed on death row. "Hanging until you die" was carried out by an unidentified hangman who wore a hood over his head. The criminal will have a rope tied around their necks while he is standing on a trap door - and then it was sprung by the hangman. The doctor will finally cut the tendon on the foot and ensuring that the person hung was dead.

My mom is remembered for her cooking, baking rum cake, sponge cake, ribbon cake and huge coconut buns. We would be chasing those cakes down with mom's home made pine apple drink, sorrel drink and ginger beer at Christmas time. Pine apples in Guyana had a strong smell and tasting sweeter than the pine apples of today. The red apples mom posted to us from the USA to Guyana in the seventies had an appetizing scent. They tasted excellent compared to the apples bought in the groceries today.

Mom had a few interesting clichés saying that "*A man and his money will soon part – when he dies he cannot take it with him*" - and other words like "*Don't be gluttonous in stuffing your mouth… Eat to live and not live to eat*". I cannot recall any of my siblings being rapacious. Our family was very charitable. And in my era, I only recognized that one can be rich while the other being poor – the middle class status was not in my vocabulary.

Our new house was built with concrete foundation and cinder blocks, wood sidings above with zinc on the roof top. When the rain falls on the window panes and the zinc roof top, it made loud noises that encouraged me, in tucking myself under the sheet in the bed awaiting the cracking of thunder and the flashing of lightening. At times, I will go outside in taking a rain bath. Surprisingly, I would see small fishes or lots of earth worms that fell from the sky or lying on the concrete and still jumping around. The rain water was safe to drink – no risk in drinking acid rain water.

My first day at a Roman Catholic school was at the age of six years old. All the kids assembled in line with their parents for registration and orientation, before being sent to their respectful class room. They would be shedding tears and wanting to return home. On settling down in my class room, I chose to make myself comfortable in the last row of benches and out of sight from the teachers. Because, I was afraid of the teachers pointing me out as the first, in answering a question before getting to the other students, in the back benches in the class room.

The teachers became my second parents. You were whipped with a wild cane when you were misbehaving or not doing your homework - a plus for the teachers, because no parent ever protested or complained when their kids were spanked with the wild cane. If you let your parents know about the whipping, your parent will also give you a whipping. And, even though we were not well off financially, I gave away my pencils every week to any kid that was in need of one.

The Catholic School had a church that the kids were introduced to. It was mandatory for all students, in attending mass on certain days of the week. I usually admire the uniforms that the altar boys had worn during the church services. The incense that was in the cistern was swung to and fro, while the altar boys were walking along the isle among the congregation. But kneeling down in the front of the church close to the altar and waiting the communion - it was not that exciting as I previously thought. The priest will be the first person, in putting his lips on the large silver cup and then taking a gulp of the red wine. He will then share the left over wine with the members that were authorized in taking communion. At times, when my turn came around in sipping the wine from the famous silver cup, and with that cup smelling funny, I would refuse in taking a sip of the wine. If there was a pretty girl next to me: Then without hesitating, I would drink the wine, even if it smelled funky or it was having lip stick on the cup. I later realized that my soared throat was contracted from sipping wine in the Catholic Church.

In attending a Catholic school and the learning's that I had received in the classroom - it made me very unsure about what was being taught in the school. With my upbringing, along with learning the British system and their way of life were complicated to me. I did not complain, but felt that I was being brainwashed into the British culture. And thence – forth I was not myself, only I was being led by foreigners in living their way of life.

My mom had a fixed daily meal schedule. – Monday through Sunday, an everlasting menu without deviating from her regular schedule. However, I personally used to be looking forward for the goodies that came after the meals. My mom would some times dish out delicious custard made with raisons and currents to everyone sitting at the table. At lunch time when all the siblings had gathered at the famous table – it looks like the Knights of the elliptical Table. At times, I would distract any of my brothers or sisters that were sitting closest to me. Whosoever turns his or her eyes away from their plate – I will then pinch their meat off their plate, before them realizing that they were duped.

Every Saturday at approximately three o'clock, a pastry vendor by the name of Mrs. Winnie would be delivering the most tasty pine tarts, coconut pone, black pudding and sugar cakes at our home. Usually, I will await her at the beginning of the street and escorting her to my mom in paying up the cash. And my mother's guava jelly or jam and the pine jelly were excellent in comparison to what was being sold in the grocery. I learned to cook, bake, doing house chores. Chores like ironing my own clothes and washing my under wears, and observing my mother on a daily basis at a very young age, became beneficial to me in latter days.

The milk that the family drank was directly from the cow. The cows only grazed in the pastures where their appropriate grass was grown. I had never seen cows eating regular food other than grass, along with drinking water - the cows were healthier and so were we. The cows in Guyana never had any mad cow diseases. The fowls that mother had bred were fed on rice paddy and water. They were also healthier and very chewable and tasty when eaten. No young girls had grown breasts before the appropriate age; and the boys did not have breasts when they had eaten the fowls from mom's pen. I can recall that a chicken is the young of a fowl and they were all yellow.

Mom planted her own kitchen garden in every inch of yard space that was available to her. All kind of vegetables that were found in the market places were sowed and reaped in our kitchen garden. I had the daily task in shoveling up dried cow dung in the pasture that was close to our home. Mom used the cow dung as manure for her kitchen garden beds. Fertilizer was not used in enhancing the growth of the plants in mom's garden. Sometimes we had excessive vegetables to be giving away to the neighbors, family or friends. My mother was not only a homemaker, but she was a good medicine woman - a dispenser of medicine and having remedies for any ailment in the family.

One day, I was walking in an alleyway, and usually a short cut to my house. I was bitten by a black lab aria snake which was approximately two feet in length. And seconds after being bitten, the venom radiated an excruciating pain throughout my entire body and giving me an instant headache. I ran home as fast I can, telling my mom what had happened. She did not become panicky, but she cracked an egg and telling me to hold my nose and swallow it. The pain immediately subsided and she took me to the public hospital for further medical treatment. My mom's quick thinking and her rendering me first aid had probably saved my life. Years followed, and I was also bitten by a scorpion while serving in the military.

All moms' children were considered her asset; and she had no difficulties in managing all nine kids along with a husband. The belt off the sewing machine was used as an aid in her rod of correction, whenever we misbehaved at home. She will then follow up with a long *epistle,* which hurts more than her lashes. She taught us in respecting our elders and each other – "*You do not walk through two people when they are conversing, but you have to walk around them*". My mom cherished and valued every piece of item in the house – no matter how aged they were. If any of us had taken a plastic container from her cabinet mom would surely miss that item, and she would not rest until it was returned.

Colonial Days

*L*ooking into how the British way of dressing with their suit and tie; and going to work in a very hot weather at ninety degrees or over – it was inappropriate, or it did not impressed me. And it never did galvanize my way of understanding what life was about.

The women wore well starched can – can that made them look like Barbie dolls, with them carrying their colorful umbrellas that they used in both summer and rainy seasons. In my sight it was hilarious when the Guyanese girls wore their starched can – cans. They look more like Donald and Daffy ducks, and more comical than the British women, because the girls in Guyana had a much higher rear than the English.

Our people emulated the habits and culture of the British, but after realizing that they were being led with a ring in their nose. Later, they started thinking in a more practical and paradoxical manner in suiting their needs, and having a more suitable life style. So, the men that were born in British Guiana subsequently came up with an idea in wearing the African dashiki or shirt jack, which was more appropriate to wear in the hot climate conditions.

In growing up, I did have a clever and imaginative insight in developing new perspectives to my challenging problems, because of my situation, and knowing that I was poorer than some kids in the neighborhood. My parents could not have afforded, in giving us the things that the well off kid's parents would have given them. So, I eventually came up with constructive ideas and practical applications, in achieving the things that would make me happy. That took my mind off the negative things, and I started thinking positive by saying to myself "I can be happy without being rich.**"**

I made many friends in the new location. My friends and I used to improvise in toy making by using other items - things like the wood guns and wooden scooters. Now in the USA and other parts of the world they have reinvented the scooter; but only manufacturing them currently with metal and not wood. Ball bearings were substituted in the place of wheels. Wooden go –carts were pushed with a long stick by a friend. The sail boats and small boats were propelled by rubber bands - in joining them together and attaching them to a home made zinc propeller. The kid's improvised telephone was made with copper wire or a string, and two tin cans were use as the telephone. The bicycle wheel rims and the car tires were used to racing in the streets. And we used an eight inches smooth stick, in pushing the tires and the bicycle rims along at a fast rate of speed. Sling shots were made with a fork from certain trees; and the leather tongues from old worn out shoes were used, in holding the stone ammunitions. And tying a long string on the tail of a dragon fly, having it flying at a distance was fun to us as kids.

At Christmas, in the darkest nights, my friends and I would purchase steel wool, tied it with copper wire, ignite it and then we would swing it around our head and body displaying a bright light for two minutes. African masquerade dancing in the street and in the yards of residents during Christmas was part of a celebration for the Afro – Guyanese people. The well off kid's parents could have afforded in dressing them up with the Lone Ranger or Roy Rogers out fits, along with fancy boots at Christmas time. The only thing that was missing was a white horse. Neighborhood organizers' group would come together on a yearly basis, in entertaining families in the community. They had donkey racing, May - pole dancing, greasy pole climbing or walking a greasy pole across a fifteen feet man made trench. It was fun in having people of different back ground and the various ethnic groups coming together and having a wonderful time without recognizing the color of your skin.

Life was very enjoyable growing up in my country Guyana. It was before the splitting up of the two main races in the country – the Indians and the blacks. But I place all the blamed on the former political leaders; Mr. Cheddie Jagan who was East Indian and Mr. Forbes Burnham who was black. They both planted a stigma, in dividing the nation before they had passed away from this world. But I am longing for the day when both political parties can join together, in cooperation and unity, in developing Guyana with her vast resources; and in making Guyana a better place to live.

Death of a Favorite Sister

I had resented the teachings in the Catholic school, but I still went along with it - only to graduate and leaving the classroom. Reading was not my hobby- I was lacking the knowledge of books, so that made me think for myself, in the things seen and through my observations. I had applied much common sense in every aspect of my life. However, my advice to the younger generation of today is to continue reading as many books as possible - because reading and understanding what you have read will be a journey in attaining knowledge, wisdom and success in the real world.

Attending Hindu weddings was something I always would be looking forward in doing. Their dishes were excellent and different from my mom's home cooking; even though my mom has some Indian in her blood. Her grandfather hailed from India and her father was mixed with white and Indian. So, my mother had known how to cook Indian dishes; but only in doing so at my adult age as I may recall. Every year my mom rented a driver with his horse drawn cart, in picking up seniors at the Dharam Salah, which was about a mile away from our home. Mom will cook in bulk, and she will feed approximately twenty male and female seniors in that day – for mom was very hospitable. When they were satisfied, I would accompany them back to their facility.

The Thom's family was the neighbors on the left, and the Excurses from Portugal were our neighbors on our right. One of the Thom's brothers fell into a tank filled with molasses while attempting, in jumping

19

down from a bridge and unto a pontoon that was travelling west in the canal. A latch which would normally be closed was left opened. When he emerged from the tank, he was looking all black from the top of his head to the tip of his boots. Boys in the hood usually walked with their personal cups, in dipping molasses from the tank on the pontoons that were being pulled by a tractor along the canal. Molasses is the bi product form burnt sugar cane when processes with fire.

One weekend and in the wee hours of the morning while the entire family was asleep, I heard dogs howling in the neighborhood. And it was very unusual to hearing all the dogs howling at the same time. My dog would howl only when I am singing or in attempting to sing in the shower. Their howling sounded like an invasion of a wolf pack.

An earthquake started with a minor trembling sensation and followed by an intense shaking of my bunk bed. For a moment, I thought it was my brother Rupert messing around on the bunk bed that we shared – but it was an actual earthquake that I was experiencing for the first time ever. No major damages to properties or any fatalities were reported the following day on the radio. And at that time we had no television available to us in the country.

My sister Patsy was the "Queen Bee" of the family and in the eyes of her many friends. Later my mom considered my younger sister Sandra as the "Queen Bee" that is, when my sister Patsy died. My eldest brother Eustace had a pellet gun known to me as an air rifle. I frequently practiced shooting with his rifle, and I became a good marksman. (i.e., after practicing on weekends when the gun was available or when my eldest brother was out of the house). In most cases, I will use a sling shot in shooting down flying gal lings and cranes; or I will use it for hunting birds further in the back dams which was located behind the cemetery. It was illegal picking the coconuts in the cemetery.

One of my friends had mounted a coconut tree- then he began picking and throwing the nuts down to us. He accidentally interrupted a bee hive nest causing a swarm of bees in attacking the gang. We ran in all direction - some of us plunging into the canal in avoiding the bee stings while others lay low in the grass. My friend in the coconut tree suffered the most bee stings. He was beyond recognition when we next saw him emerging out of the bushes.

I had a notion that of anything my friend can do I could have done better, and I was always competitive. I once tried smoking an improvised cigarette which I had made out of brown paper and coconut fiber. When I lit the cigarette, it instantaneously turned into fire ball, gushing upwards and burning my lips. Since then, I did not again attempt imitating my father or tried to be a copy cat smoking cigarettes; or ever again tried to be like my friends that smoked cigarettes.

My eldest brother Eustace had a very creative mind. He had given the family high hopes in becoming rich over night. Eustace had dug a hole in the ground at the front of the house, pouring kerosene oil into the hole and claiming that he had struck oil. He caused my mom the expense, in buying more than the usual amount of kerosene. At first, the family thought that he may have been on to something spectacular – and it giving us very high hopes in becoming wealthy. But as time went on, it was discovered that he was playing us all along. Eustace was somewhat tenacious and was very serious into making model aero planes. At times we would both go into the open field, in flying his self built wooden model plane that never lasted two seconds in the air without crashing to the ground in a nose dive. At one time, Eustace brought his post office buddy to our home in challenging me in boxing. Within seconds after him putting on the gloves I knocked him down. My mom had to render first aid, in giving him smelling salts.

Some of us in the family had a nickname. I used to get very angry when one of my younger brothers called me by my nickname instead of addressing me by my given name. A destitute relationship was among the brothers in the family, but each of us had a strong sense of our own identity and special skills - we however respected each other. My eldest brother has kept in contact with our relative, but I did not. It was embarrassing at times when going out to parties befriending young ladies, and not knowing that they were related to you, until when striking up a conversation and giving them my true name. But most occasions, I will give girls a false name. When they recognize me in the streets, they will call out to me, but I would not respond, because I will forget the name that I had given them.

As a teenager, I frequented parties during the week, and sometimes every weekend with my friends. I had known the latest dance steps going back to the eighties. I got into many fights on the dance floor, because I would be holding someone's girl friend far too close for comfort - in doing slow dancing in the dark corner of the floor and wearing my sun glasses at night.

Wanna-bee Altar Boy

My next door neighbor to the right of us was Portuguese – and he was a few years older than me. Dennis's nick name was "Sad Sack." He was a member of the Roman Catholic Church of altar boys. I was very enthusiastic in joining the group and becoming an altar boy - but things did not work out for me. The journey started when Dennis was taking me to the Parson of the church in enrolling me as an altar boy. We were riding a bicycle over a narrow muddy creek and both of us fell into a ditch - emerging from the ditch very dirty, smelly mud all over our body and clothes. An East Indian woman came to the rescue of Dennis, but she completely ignored me as if I was a phantom. Never did she render any assistance to me. She took Mr. Muddy Dennis inside her house; giving him a bath and dry clothes to wear. Also washing his muddy clothes and putting them to dry, while I was awaiting him on the dam, in order for him in accompanying me back home. It was very conspicuous that the Indian woman showed more preference to my Portuguese friend.

On arriving at home, the dried mud on my clothes and skin made me look like a mummy. My mom actually did not recognize her own son. She did not quarrel nor did she say anything to me, but only escorting me into the shower in getting rid of the stench and the dried mud. To my surprise she left; returning with a machine belt and giving me some lashes while the water was still running. It stung more than her regular lashes when it is dry. All this drama occurred because I wanted to become a wanna – bee altar boy in the Catholic Church.

I have closed the door on most of my treasured past - not for me, but for the sake of my children or children's children. But some things in my memoir are good for thoughts to the youths of today, in understanding that they cannot get away with breaking the law. *Youths should be aware, that the integrity of a righteous person shall guide them. But the perverseness of transgressors shall destroy them.* Others chapters in this book have interesting recommendations in becoming some body important in a community or society. Reading any literatures or novels was not my type of hobby. In most cases I will pick up a news paper and reading only the headlines. I loved reading comic books like Superman, Batman, Captain Marvel, Rip Kirby, Lone Ranger, Wonder Woman, Roy Rogers, and Pop – Eye, Archie, and with others that I cannot remember.

My classmate Douglas, one of the boys in the neighborhood met with other friends in going into the cane field in cutting the burnt out sugar cane. We did accomplish our mission to a certain extent, but we were surprisingly ambushed by a ranger who was mounted on a black horse. He was armed with a shot gun that was loaded with rice paddy pellets. We did not spot him on time, because all of us had a large bundle of sugar cane on our heads - like a horse bridle with our eyes were focused to the front. However, we all scattered in various directions when the ranger began chasing us - in that he can chase only one of us at a time. But the ranger chose to go after Douglas as his lottery - firing his shot gun with paddy pellets. I suddenly heard Douglas screaming for help, but there was nothing else any of the other boys could have done in saving him – every man was for himself. Finally, Douglas caught up with us - that is, when we crossed the canal with our bundle of cane on our head. Actually, I told the boys to wait for him. He was not shot, but he told us a story that the ranger had given him a break.

A Family's Tragedy

*I*n the sixties and in my immediate neighborhood, the girls participated in all sorts of sport activities with the boys. The British had introduced a game called rounder's. When the ball was pitched the batter will strike the ball, and then run in a circle to a marker in the dirt – similar to a base ball game played in America and elsewhere. Maybe it was copied from the British Rounder's.

It was a very sad and touching story about a family's tragedy involving two of my neighbor's beautiful daughters who were friends of mine. And one rainy day, they left home in purchasing stuff at the grocery store. On returning from the grocery store, the younger girl stopped to wash her muddy feet at the aqueduct, because it was raining heavily on that day. She then lost her balance and fell overboard. The older sister panicked by jumping in the aqueduct, in attempting to save her sister – even though, neither of the two were swimmers and they both drowned. The tragic news got to their mother's attention. Immediately she came down with an acute stroke, paralyzing the entire right side of her body. In my community there were no swimming pools or swimming instructors, in giving swimming lessons to the youths in our neighborhood. We learned swimming techniques on our own in the nearby dirty trenches or canal. It resulted that most of us contracted ring worm on our body.

One Saturday morning while I was passing by the Catholic Church a large crowd had gathered in the street, and they were curiously looking in the direction of the church.

Curiosity caught my attention which caused me in joining the crowd. I learned from someone in the crowd that demons were throwing candle stick lamps, the cistern and with other utensils at the priest, while he was with his altar boys rehearsing in the church for the Sunday morning mass. Since after that incident, I did not allow anyone in convincing me in doing something that I did not appreciate. However, it went on for a period of time until the police squad car came and entered the church. This particular incident really did discourage me from joining the Catholic Church. Subsequently, my mother encouraged me and my sister Patsy in enrolling in the Anglican Church which was approximately two miles away from our home. We both started going to the confirmation classes on Saturdays. My mom had given us her bicycle so that I can take my sister to the confirmation classes.

Deliberately, one Saturday I stayed away from the class, because I found that the Anglican churches teaching practices were no different from the Catholic Church. The following Saturday when we reported for classes the priest took off my pants, benching me over a desk in the presence of my sister and giving me twelve lashes with his broad belt. That was my final confirmation class in the churches.

Music Selection

The type of music and songs I had enjoyed dancing with the girls at parties was by Otis Redding, *"Sitting on the dock of the bay,"* The Drifters; Wilson Pickett; Jimmy Cliff; Percy Sledge *"When a man loves a woman"*; Bob Marley; songs of the sixties, Soca music and later songs of the eighties. Any other boring music, I would have passed in sitting out next to the juke box and falling asleep in the party. I actually started going to many parties after graduating from Elementary and attending a Secondary school - my sister Patsy also went to the same school. I was nominated a School Prefect in enforcing school rules on students that were not adhering to school policies and procedures - as they were stipulated by the Headmaster of the school.

One day, I had placed my sister in detention, in not wearing the prescribed school beret and while she was walking in the street on her way to school. After my sister's detention, Patsy started challenging me in every possible subject at school. She was very competitive with me, but she was more intelligent than I was. I was more involved into playing sports and flirting with the girls. I was definitely confused with my priorities.

We both walked approximately two miles to and from school on a daily basis. Most times I ran home during my lunch hour, but returning back to school on time in taking up my prefect position. It enables me in becoming a good athlete.

An incident that stuck in my mind during a school hour break - it was a fight between two pretty and bright girls in my class. They were fighting in an empty class room located on the first floor of the school. Hol was a very quiet and lady like girl. During the altercation, she however got the better of her opponent who was more pugnacious and provocative. She ripped off the girl's brazier and exposing a bunch of rolled up news paper that fell out from the girl's brazier. So, the breast the boys were lusting over was not for real. It was very embarrassing to the other girl who was thence forth teased by the boys in the class room.

A beginning of a new Life

Both my parents came to the United States of America working and sending back monies, processed food and clothes home to all nine children. Later, my sister Patsy became ill with jaundice – a disease which caused her eyes and finger nails in becoming yellow. She was eventually hospitalized after being convinced by the rest of siblings in seeking medical treatment. My parents returned home in taking care of Patsy while she was hospitalized – but Patsy later died. Patsy's boy friend was also admitted in the same hospital. He came down with an acute pneumonia. He was in the ward directly above hers and mysteriously died on the said day. Strangely around 5:00 am that morning prior to my sister's death; my mom dreamt that two angels had ascended escorting my sister. She had told me that said morning moments before leaving for the hospital.

The doctor and nurses confirmed that it was the said time at 5:00 am that she had died. Her sudden death came as a shock to me, also to all her friends, relatives and family. I didn't attend Patsy's funeral, because I was bruised from a previous motor cycle accident. However, the funeral possession of cars was passing by our home on the day of her funeral. It was a custom in showing respect to the deceased. Our dog Rex started howling until the last car went by.

Because of my traumatic state of mind, and from that day on, my life style and high hopes in life started going down hill. I began living one day at a time, believing that my life also will be cut short. I placed education on hold and started living as if it was the beginning of the first day for the rest of my life. But life as I was thinking will be completed by setting early goals and objectives, and determining the course of my actions for the future that I had wanted it to be. I did eventually identify my inner strengths by tapping into the hidden talents and my capabilities that I possessed. I did pray to the Almighty God in helping me getting through a good life without a formal education. For my parents could not have afforded in sending nine children to college with their low income.

Before returning to the USA, my mom left her car entrusted in my care. It made me more popular in the eyes of friends, because the car was their ticket in us going partying on the weekends. Actually, before she had left for the USA, I learned to drive her car on my own. When my mom was taking her daily nap at around 1:00 pm, I would crawl on my belly, getting under her pillow and taking the car keys. Then, I will push the car out into the main street before starting the engine. I had experienced that when you have something attractive – it draws more friends closer to you. And when you do not have anything special, no one wants to be your best friend.

One stormy night, I overloaded the car with some teenage friends including a few girls. While I was driving to the city to a party, the wind shield wiper malfunctioned. I turned down the window on the right, using my right hand as a wind shield wiper so that I can have a clear vision on the road. In my country driving on the left hand side of the road is legal, because the driver's seat is on the right. I believe most countries in Europe are doing the same. When I came to USA, I made a mistake in driving on the left side of the road, nearly causing a serious accident. That said night I heard a big bang outside the party. Then, one of my friends came running into the party immediately notifying me that someone had just hit my car. The car was parked in the street, but the driver sped away with his own car. When I came down examining the car, there was only a tiny scratch on the car rear chrome bumper. If it were the cars of today that is being made with plastic body and clips; one third of the rear of the car would have been scattered all over the street due to that impact of the other hit and run vehicle.

The Bullies

For fighting with bullies was a satisfactory kind of sport that I always be looking forward in doing - especially on a Friday afternoon and on my way home after classes was dismissed. Surprisingly, a very good friend of mine challenged me in a fight after school recess. The reason being that he started bullying a couple of students in the school. He had changed his attitude towards me - from being a humble person to an audacious character. I started boxing at the age of twelve years old, and I became a very good street fighter. He was bigger in size but slower than me. So, that when he threw punches, he was unable in landing them on me - only because I was faster on my feet and my hands. He then picked up a stone, pelting it and causing a cut over my eye. He cowardly took off from the scene and feeling ashamed in the presence of a crowd of students. I started fighting bullies since I was in Catholic school. When some of my quietest and nerdy class mates had taken a low hair cut; the bullies would hit them at the back of the head. When they make complaints to the teachers, the gang will await them after school, and taking turns in tapping them behind the head.

I can fluently read in Spanish and speak a little of the language. And taking my finals in the secondary school - it was not that exciting to me. It was not something that I was not looking forward in doing; because I was still grieving the death of my sister who was only one year younger than me. Deliberately, I absented myself from the examination center in two of the subjects out of the eight which I had signed up for. They

31

were Geometry and Literature. The day of reckoning came the senior students crowded the hallway of the school by the principle's office and looking at the bulletin board for their results. At the said time, I was passing by and saw a few of the girls crying, because they had failed their final exam. One of my friends told me, that I had passed five of the subjects taken – I was not the least excited about the results.

Mainly sports were my thing in school. My favorite sports are presently boxing, soccer, table tennis, cricket, swimming, badminton, racket ball, shooting pool, track and field. I am currently a licensed USA amateur boxing and physical fitness coach; and sometimes sparing partner for amateur boxers. Also, I had done some training with my friends, in obstacle training in preparation for the famous nation - wide Spartan Race.

Boys Will Be Boys

Soon after Guyana had gained its independence in the year 1967, the prime minister and the government had banned all imported food items coming into the country. It became illegal for the stores or any citizen of Guyana, in having contraband items on the shelves or in their houses. However, the merchants found a way in saving their businesses. The rest of the population had done the same in order to survive. Some people illegally crossed over into neighboring countries like Surinam, Venezuela and Brazil in the hours of darkness, in purchasing band goods. Our household did not miss these band items. The canned goods were not frequently bought by my parents. And we survived off of farinaceous meals as: rice; flour; sago; cassava and various types of ground provisions from mom's kitchen garden. Once a week my dad on his way home from the night shift will bring home fresh fish from the fishermen's trawler and toasted bread from the bakery.

An issue that had taken place in the seventies has stuck in my mind. It's a mysterious fire of stables and horses at a very famous race track. It was one of my favorite sports that I attended every Saturday – that is, horse racing on the race track. The race track was owned by a very prominent lawyer by the name of Lionel Luckoo. Mysteriously, the stable and horses were burnt in a fire – not in determining its origin as per the investigation findings of the fire and the reports from police departments. Since then, there were no more horse racing or gambling in the area of the track, which was frequented by many people in the city.

My first job after leaving school was working at Bookers Drug as a chemist. I received on the job training in under studying a co – worker. However, I resigned from that job after I accidentally burnt myself with a compound that made the cough medicine. My other job was at the Ministry of Economic Development working as a messenger and an office assistant. I worked there for a period of eight months and then joining the police force. Prior to me joining the force, I was arrested a couple of times – one for sitting on a skid, while a bulldozer was dragging the houses and relocating them to another location. The next time arrested was at a scene of a burnt out jewelry store. It was after planning with my friend Collie, in going searching for gold in the burned building's ground floor. The cops showed up and caught us red handed with a few fake gold items in our pockets. We were taken to the Police Station lockups and awaited our parents in taking us home – no bail was posted.

Prior to me joining the police force – as a kid I broke the law on a few other occasions. My friends and I had nothing else in doing when school closed during the summer break. We normally gambled with a deck of cards for cents and pennies in the back yard of a friend's house. The cops frequently made their raids on us, that is, when the neighbors call the 999 police emergencies. I then planned and organized with my friend in setting a trap for the police officers whenever they had shown up to our gambling site. And at the rear of the yard in the range houses, the women usually hung their clothes out to dry on wire lines. I disconnected one of the lines from a pole, by dropping it to the ground in a concealed manner, but out of sight from the police officers. They showed up in a Black Mariah Van, thinking that they had the element of surprise on us – but this time we were prepared for them. When they came charging blindly in the back yard – one of my friends who lived in one of the ranges, held an end of the clothes line in his house, then pulling it on my signal and tripping a few of the officers. We then ran through another friend's house into the front street and cleanly got away from the cops.

When I became older I had made a vow that when I do join the police force, and if I am not promoted within four years I would quit the force. Because my dad was a police corporal on the force for many years before he had a promotion. The British had an unfair system established in the country which caused the promotions of Guianese police officers to be stagnated. But a British born citizen employed on the force was rapidly promoted. So, in joining the police force, I had pledge an allegiance in upholding the laws of my country under all circumstances. I told my mom jokingly that if she ever breaks the law I will arrest her and then post bail for her release.

Prior to the country gaining independence, a police recruit had to be six feet tall in enlisting on the force. That policy was however changed when the country had gained independence in 1967. The fire department and the police force were merged as one entity. I realized that being a rookie cop; at times one had to deal with situations in a rational, objective and tactful manner, but I always trusted my common sense and judgments. Also, I have the ability in effectively analyzing relevant information and essential facts of a matter, when solving a crime or a major problem. At times a police officer has to use diplomacy and some psychology, in calming down situations and in making peace especially during a domestic dispute.

My first assignment was working the beat on the day shift – from 7:00 am to 3:00 pm tour. I stopped a rider on a bicycle when he failed in adhering to a stop sign. All I wanted to do was to give him a warning. I did just that, but he showed his appreciation by quickly putting ten dollars into my top pocket of my uniform and riding away.

In the Police Training Academy, we were not taught anything thing about taking gifts from anyone at anytime on duty. But I felt guilty to this day, in accepting money from that gentleman – even though it was not intentional or premeditated in taking money from anyone. Then, I became more aware of my duties as a police officer, when I started interacting with people in the streets. And as a patrolman, I realized that one must have a high level of curiosity, coupled with a strong power of observation. A police officer's third eye is his mind. He or she must demonstrate the ability in analyzing problems, obtaining relevant information and essential facts from witnesses. What I did learn about talking with eye witnesses in cases of accidents or crimes. Each witness will give a different version in what had taken place and not giving the exact time of the occurrence. This happens if each witness had seen the accident or a crime from different angles; or not viewing it at the said time of the occurrence.

Domestic violence in the city of Georgetown was an everyday occurrence. It involved both spouses that inflicted bodily harm on each other. But the majority of domestic violence cases had involved the men; only about one percent involving the women assaulting their husbands. At times when the husband is arrested, the women will plea for his release or she will not show up in court the case. And the reason being is that she has no other source of income or financial assistance for her children if he goes to jail.

I had achieved my perfection and techniques in communicating clearly, forcefully, effectively with the credibility and confidence to the public. It was by asking penetrating questions from the witnesses or even a suspect in a crime.

My first arrest on the job as a rookie cop was involving a matter in domestic violence between a husband and wife at their home. Being a rookie cop, I was very flamboyant and enthusiastic in making my first arrest, and wanting to show a good first impression of myself in the eyes of my superiors. So, when I approached the scene, I heard loud voices coming from a man and a woman. I walked up the stairs, which was located on the outside of the building, and I knocked on the door. When the man opened up and letting me into the house; I observed broken ceramic plates scattered on the floor and the house was in total disarray. Being smaller in size and five feet ten inches tall and with the man six feet tall or over – he used me with profanities. When he placed his hand on me, I quickly wrestled him to the floor. We both found ourselves rolling down a long stairs and into the yard. I then placed him into a choke hold, spraying him with mace until he had given up. When the man recovered, I cuffed him and we both walked to the station. While in the lockup, he apologized to me for his behavior. However,

I did charge him for assaulting a police officer and domestic violence against his wife in the home.

On most occasions, I have made sound or difficult and unpopular decisions when facing adversities, but avoiding in getting irrational. Sometimes, I will use the most objective evaluation when arriving at a scene – which means that I will imaginarily extended the scene of a crime to a few block radius. I usually kept a keen eye out for any suspicious person that is running away from the area or walking at a fast pace. Even any suspicious persons in the neighborhood that are close to the crime scene on my approach…

My superiors had trusted me being a good cop in the streets. And I judiciously carried out my assignments without receiving any instructions or directions from my headquarters. I always capture all opportunities with the eagerness, in trying new approaches by using psychology in calming down a situation – regardless the volition or the complexity of the occurrences. On my off days from the job, I frequent the Criminal Investigation Division; asking the sergeant in charged permission in doing case studies of all known criminals in the city, and their modus operandi. And I became familiar with criminal faces, their home addresses and where they hung out.

My biggest case was involving a jewelry hoist in the heart of the city on a very busy day and time. We had just received a call on the radio while patrolling in our squad car. My regular partner was off duty on that day, so I had a substitute partner working with me. The report that came in was that a motor cycle gang had stormed into a jewelry store, breaking a few show cases; stealing thousands of dollars worth of jewelries and sped away on motor cycles.

In those days, not too many people were owners of motor cycles, or could have afforded one. Honda was the only model and brand of motor cycles in the country. But I had an idea where the motor cycle gang was hanging out. So, we proceeded to the warlock neighborhood, in observing six ladies Honda motor cycles parked in the drive way. I then placed my hand on one of the motor cycle exhaust pipe, and it was very hot. Immediately, I radio my operation room for back up. In kicking open the front door of the house and using the element of surprise - we arrested two suspects while the others ran out through the back exit door and into a cane field. My partner monitored the two men that were handcuffed in the patrol car, while I proceeded in searching the house for the stolen jewelries. I found some of the jewelries in a pot with boiling rice and beans, some under the rug, but most of them were found in an overhead toilet tank on the upper floor. All the jewelries were recovered that day. And later the other suspects were captured in the cane field by the Police Special Unit.

A Good Cop

As a rookie cop, I was very much alert. I always think before taking any action and in using a more common sense approach, intelligent reasoning and mental toughness – a must combination while facing danger. Being audacious will not make one an effective cop. Most of my partners working patrol with me in the squad car were twice my size, but they were not having the courage in pursuing dangerous criminal – or fearing retribution from the criminals especially when they are off duty. Georgetown is a small city with only a few movie theaters or other places in taking the family to social events when off duty. Some officers were afraid of being accosted by a criminal that they had previously arrested in the street. Officers are always at risk with their lives, twenty four hours and seven days a week because they were not allowed in taking home their fire arms, but having to deposit it in the arms room. I was characterized by many as fearless in doing my duties as a police officer in the streets. In this twenty first century, I learned that the criminals are now carrying AK-47 rifles in my country; versus some of the police officers who are armed with service revolvers. But some other officers do carry rifles in the city or when they are carrying out special operations.

In another occurrence involving a situation at the Registrar Office where I had received my marriage license – a man had an altercation with a staff member, because of a personal dispute with that worker. He was being boisterous along with his disorderly behavior. So he had attracted many workers attention on the floor, causing a temporary halt to the operations in the various departments. On reporting to the scene, I stayed in the car because I believed that it was only a minor incident, and it would not have taken too long. My partner went up to the floor investigating the report, but he took some time before reporting back to me. So I left the car and proceeded to the floor, in finding my partner standing within the crowd, looking at the man threatening the workers and not taking any action. So, I immediately approached the man, rugby tackling him to the floor, hand cuffing him and taking him into custody.

A good police officer should maintain public order in a very tactful manner when applying or enforcing the law. Also, the officer's duty is to protect life and property from the preposterous or pugnacious type of people in the streets of Georgetown. As a cop in those days, I had never shot anyone or had any reason in doing so. But in the big cities in the USA, a very small percentage of cops will shoot someone, because of his and her instincts or having the license in taking a human life. Using deadly force on someone must be justified – either in saving someone's life or the life of their own. If that's not the case, a police officer shall not concoct their evidence or should be hiding the real truth of the matter. *Some will sleep not, except they have done mischief and evil, causing someone to fall.*

Juvenile Delinquents

Gold chain snatching was very rampant in the city of Georgetown. Most of the victims were old ladies going to or coming from the churches; or the girls donned in their expensive jewelries on their way off to a party or elsewhere. One Sunday morning, a juvenile delinquent snatched a gold neck chain from off an old lady coming from church service. I always study the zones thoroughly in which I would be working on that day, (i.e. incase I have to chase a suspect on foot or in giving chase to an assailant in my squad car). That morning, it paid off well as the perpetrator ran through a church compound which was approximately a block long. I was waiting for him in the street and just under a seven feet concrete wall. He surprisingly jumped on the hood of the patrol car. He was immediately apprehended - and the victim's gold chain was recovered intact.

A police officer assigned in driving a patrol car has to be an expert driver with the skills in maneuvering his squad car during a chase. They must be able in driving at a very high rate of speed, going forward or driving in the reverse mode. And one evening, I was on car patrol and I received a call from the operation room that a man was threatening to kill his wife with a machete in her home. On arrival at the scene, I saw a man quickly entering his car. I put on my emergency lights, signaling him not to drive off, but he ignored my signal by speeding away at a fast rate of speed. I gave chase, going over sixty miles an hour and beating all stop signs in the streets of Georgetown. Eventually, I caught up with the assailant, that is, when he lost control of his car and ended up in a lower embankment off the road. When I approached the suspect, he was disoriented and not cognizant of what was taking place. The man had over three thousand dollars in cash. I cuffed him and took him to the hospital for treatment to his bruises. Subsequently, the full amount of his cash was returned to him.

My choice of shift was working from 11:00 pm to 7:00 am. I had volunteered in working on the weekends and during the dark hours for one reason – in catching criminals in the act of committing a crime and especially the ones that committed burglary. I found that they come out after 12:30 am in the wee hours in the morning in committing their crime. Normally, I would be driving the squad car without the head lights on - merely in sneaking up on criminals unexpectedly. Most time criminals do work in pairs – one always being on the lookout for the other. One morning at 2:00 am while on car patrol, I observed two shadows in the dark and a few blocks. Without my headlights beaming down in the street, I drove at an idling speed catching up with the suspects. One of the suspects was carrying a very large tarpaulin on his head. It was the property of the cricket board. Neither of the two suspects had noticed the car approaching.

That week a cricket team from India was in Guyana playing the West Indies cricket team in a World Series match. Usually, after play had concluded for the day, the officials will cover the field with a huge tarpaulin in case of rain. I drove up touching one suspect with my car bumper. He then dropped the stolen property and ran into a yard in a residential neighborhood – a neighborhood that I was well acquainted with. The fowls began crackling in their pen, indicating that they were being disturbed. When I approached, I saw the perpetrator in a crouching position and with the fowls gathering on one side in the pen. The suspect was then arrested and taken into custody.

Being a police officer in my country definitely calls for profiling someone acting in a suspicious manner. And if a group of teenagers or adults are loitering at a corner at nights and after midnight. At times, officers will dragnet every one standing at the corner or elsewhere. Or while engaging in the drag netting; in some instances, a decent youth may be too close to a crowd, and he will also be caught in that snare.

Once a month, the operating team of police officers will have a crackdown in arresting many suspects or criminals wanted in past and serious crimes. At a road block, a squad of police officers will be stopping a vehicle and driver for minor traffic offences, in not having a valid driver's license, or sometimes a vehicle may be stolen. At times, a police officer will discover that the driver or passengers may have outstanding warrants in their arrest. They may also be carrying contraband items or guns in the trunk of their vehicle. In my country of Guyana, a police officer will remain in his vehicle when making a stop on another vehicle. An officer will tell the driver and passengers to disembark the vehicle – in placing their hands on their head and leaning against the vehicle. Both officers will then cautiously approach the suspects vehicle from two angles - one going to the left, and while the other will be going to right of the suspects. When there are two officers, the suspects will then be patted down from the top to the bottom - it including their foot wears and headdress.

Early one morning while driving without an operator, I observed a male approaching my squad car in a dark street without a functioning street light. He had in his possession one bicycle pump, which was tucked under his armpit. I stopped, asking him to hand over the item to me, and he did so on my command. On examining the pump, it was discovered that he had installed a long knife in the handle of the pump. Without a doubt the perpetrator had had bad intentions, in committing a serious criminal act that early morning. For a police officer working in the streets especially at nights- it's a very dangerous job. Within a split second the officer has to be very volitional. A criminal can take the life of an officer when they are making a stop. A police officer's bounded duty is to be very observant at all times, either on or off duty. A cop has to posses a strong ability in remembering numbers, a complete description of a suspect from the head to the toes; and in recalling events in a chronological order. He or she must be familiar with the people in the community, schools, vendors, churches and managers in the work places. So that when a serious crime is committed, the police officer will have the full co- operation of the people in the community.

It was a blackout night when I was patrolling a very bad area with a substitute partner. We spotted a suspect carrying a bag over his shoulder. On approaching, he ran into a dark alleyway. We gave chase, but my partner stumbled and fell behind me, discharging a round from his service revolver. Immediately, I aborted the chase in helping my partner who was in shock before getting to his feet.

While on car patrol we got a radio call from the Headquarters that a naked man was in the middle of the street stopping the traffic and disturbing the peace. On approaching, the suspect spotted us and ran away in attempting to scale a fence. My partner pulled out his service revolver, fatally shooting the man in the back and leaving the man hanging on the fence. My partner knowing that he was wrong in his actions – wanted me to cover up for him in concocting my report in stating that the suspect had attacked him and he had acted in self defense. I wrote my report telling exactly what had taken place at the scene – and it was definitely murder. The officer was subsequently charged and was dismissed from the police force.

In my country, it was a standing protocol that two officers will respond to a crime scene or a domestic dispute. However, on that day the station was out by two officers, so the station sergeant sent one officer on foot, in investigating a domestic dispute which was one block away from the station. According to a written report received from the officer who had responded to the scene on that day. It stated that when he arrived at the scene, he was accosted by a male in a house, who was weighing about two hundred and fifty pounds. The man aggressively and in a menacing manner brandished a machete at the officer, causing the officer in defending himself by picking up a chair in the house. The machete somehow sliced through the bar of the chair and wounding the officer in the center of his forehead.

In receiving a call that an officer was down, I immediately arrived at the scene on foot. When I approached the man I did not ask him any questions, but I tackled him to the floor, and wrestling the machete out of his hands. He was placed in custody and charged with aggravated assault, causing serious bodily harm to an officer, resisting arrest and domestic violence. The officer was taken to the emergency room for trauma and treatment to his wound.

A mother's Fear

*I*n the city of Georgetown some places are known for their violence. If anyone other than the residence that is living in Alboystown had ventured through the hood, they were ominously looking to be beaten up or robbed. I had known a steel pan player that was living in the Alboystown neighborhood. I was also a steel pan player, and I played in the police steel band as a guitar pan player. The police steel band played at many institutions, including an isolated institution where they housed leprosy patients. I had known this street fighter, because our band had entered a competition against their band a few times. Albert was known for his fist fighting skills to many youths in other bad neighborhoods, namely Warlock and Hell's Kitchen.

On a sunny day while patrolling close to the town, I received a radio call from my Headquarters dispatching me to a scene in Alboystown. On arrival at the scene, I saw Albert sitting on the ground and holding his intestines in his hands. He was cognizant of his surroundings and appearing to me that he will pull through his ordeal. Eyewitnesses reported that a gang member from another neighborhood was fist fighting with Albert, but the man was getting the worst of it. The man then pulled out a jaw bone of an ass, slashing Albert in the lower abdomen. I had a good look at the wound. And what I saw, was half of Albert's guts protruding out, and somewhat covered with saw dusts. I did not wait for the arrival of an ambulance, but immediately placing him in the back seat of the patrol car, and driving him to the hospital's emergency room. Albert was admitted, but died about four hours later in the Operating Room.

Violence and preposterous behavior in Guyana is no difference from the violence elsewhere across the globe. The world is a violent place that we all live in, and with some people not having any empathy for others. A criminal will kill someone for a dollar or even when venturing unto another gang's turf. As a law officer working in maintaining law and order, it must be acknowledged that those police officers are not judges or jury in the streets or elsewhere. But sometimes a police officer is required to use deadly force, that is, when it is absolutely necessary in doing so. But in some instances when officers are confronted by a mentally deranged person; he or she must have the skills, in recognizing behavioral patterns and in dealing with such case in the appropriate way - as per the written laws. However, an officer is the one that has to be flexible sometimes, in making a judgment call based on the situation. An officer has to display a very high standard of professionalism and values. He has to be physically fit on the job at all times. Continuing physical training, refreshing course with the laws and procedures are a requirement of all officers in participating on an annual basis. Officers have to prepare themselves, in demonstrating intellectual inquisitiveness at a scene and during the investigation at a crime scene.

Every year in Guyana, the Hindu celebrates a festival what is known as Pagwah. On that festive day, colorful water - preferable mixed with red dye is thrown on passersby, or friends in the neighborhood. On that very Pagwah day I was on static century at the bedside in the public hospital and guarding a handcuffed criminal. Suddenly, there was confusion in the ward where I was on duty. Some neighbors drove a man to the hospital all the way from the East Coast, approximately ten mile away from the city hospital. They brought the man in a bloody rice bag. When he was removed from the bag by the hospital orderlies, I observed that he was severely wounded on the head, shoulders, hands, knees and ankles — but he somewhat survived his ordeal. Information received that the man had thrown red dye on someone's wife who was dressed in white clothes - this causing the woman's irate husband, in mincing him up from the head to the ankle with the machete.

My mom had fears in me getting killed due of my assertiveness while executing an arrest on criminals – along with the stories that people told her. What my mother did not realize is that I had strong interpersonal skills, in promoting relationships of trust, with the man in the street by: Displaying honesty; genuineness and respect in dealing with others, especially people of various cultural and background.

It can be very difficult in understanding how the man in the street is thinking. A police officer can be called at anytime in making an arrest when on or off duty or even while vacationing somewhere in the country side. A police officer had to be acquainted with the people in his community so that when he needs any assistance, in solving a crime committed in that neighborhood, the kids and adults will give him full cooperation in solving their case as previously stated. If he is rogue cop, the man in the street will be very fallacious, in giving out any tangible information to that officer. And no one will be willing in coming forward to helping him in any way or means. So, that officer will be considered an enemy in the community.

However, ninety nine percent of police officers are dedicated to their job. They will follow protocols and the law when executing their daily duties. They do not legislate or interpret the law, but uphold the law. When I was a police officer, I would give kids candies in getting their cooperation and obtaining information to solving some cases. Respecting everyone in the streets of Georgetown and at the same time being color blinded to the color of their skin, religion or sex. It was always there with me while executing my bounded duties as a good and well respected officer of the law and community. It is not the officers who have their own modus operandi, self interest, hate, or vengeance. They are the ones that have given the public a bad impression of the entire police force. An officer should never take the law in his own hand or be that bias in performing his duty. Taking calculated risks and not foreseeing your actions when making a life or death decision – it is that choice for the officer to make in evaluating their decision in that split second.

I was alone in a car patrol in a dark street when I saw a shadow scaling a fence in a residential neighborhood. Immediately I stopped the car, but forgetting to place it park before I proceeded in chasing the suspect. I n looking back I saw my patrol car following me down the street. I then realizing my mistake in not placing the car in park - I ceased chasing the suspect; then immediately jumping into the car and bringing it to a halt just in front of a ditch.

Historical Moment

I was promoted on the spot to the rank of corporal and a recipient of a policeman of the year award - it was after serving on the force for three years. It was history that was created in my country, in having the youngest police officer ever promoted in such a short period of time. That is, from a rank of constable to the rank of a corporal. It was as a surprise to me, even though I had set my goals for such an occasion. The night in question, I was playing in the police steel band at a ceremony that was about to take place in the police compound headquarters. A senior officer instructed me to getting changed into my police uniform and reporting back to the compound. A first time awards for the best policeman and policewoman of the year was held at the headquarters - and I became a recipient of such an award. No policewoman had the credentials fitting the criteria in receiving such honorable and historical award that year.

After my promotion, I was then placed in charged of the 7:00 am shift, along with seven squad cars, drivers and operators. But entropy developed within the ranks of subordinate officers in the Operation Room where I was stationed, and was in charge of a section of police officers from 7:00 am to 3:00 pm shift. One morning, when I had reported for duty, having done a roll call and dispatching the men to their area of responsibility - they suddenly came back up to the Operation Room, reporting that their patrol car tires were slashed. This enabled them in proceeding on their routine patrols. I then made a rational decision, that my shift operators will drive the squad cars, which were used on the night shift – something that was prohibited in the operation protocols manual. The incident was subsequently investigated by the Criminal Investigation Division. It revealed that one of the audacious subordinates that worked the night shift was the one responsible in sabotaging the patrol cars; and causing a delay in dispatching the men on their routine patrols.

Some time later in the year, a person or persons came by my house while I was at work and they threw some rocks – shattering a couple of glass windows in the house. No police officer was authorized in giving out my address or information to a civilian. The jealousy came about, because most of the subordinates were my seniors on the force and for a period of twelve years or over.

Policing is not only arresting a criminal or others for misdemeanor offences, but they have to display a well – oriented professional knowledge in the communities. A police officer has to show concerns for the safety of the citizens and others, in maintaining a high degree of professionalism while participating in the community. Teaching students in the schools and other centers in how to evade or prevent themselves from being a victim to a crime should be the responsibility of a community police officer. An example in evading or preventing oneself, in becoming a victim to a crime is to walk in pairs late hours at night or on a lonely street. If you noticed that you are being followed, increase your walking pace or stop in at a nearby Fire House. If there is anyone in the neighborhood or walking by: Form a conversation with them, or walk into someone's yard pretending it's your own. When walking by yourself late at night and from a distance you observed that three young men approaching – cross over the other side of the street. If they decided to split up: Turn around and get out of the neighborhood as quickly as possible.

National Service

Honesty is the best policy in every thing that you do and in every place you go – either at work or in a hotel room. Soon after working the night shift and on my way home, I was walking along a passageway to my house which was situated at the rear. I observed a brown torn paper bag with something glittery – it was on the right side of the boardwalk. On checking the bag I discovered that thousands of dollars worth of jewelries- some of them were scattered about and lying in the grass. I gathered them all up and showed them to my landlord. The landlord was astounded by me recovering all her jewelries. But then realizing that her maid had stolen the jewelries, in throwing them out of the window, so as to pick them up later when she was off duty. The landlord immediately gave the maid her walking papers.

Prior being transferred to the National Service, I was in training, in becoming a prosecutor in misdemeanor cases in the Magistrate Courts. The training lasted for six months, before the senior ranks in the police force and the Government officials had recognized that it would have been necessary, in seconding me to a new initiative that they had introduced. It was a National Service training camp for university students. I was the first instructor sent to a location out of the city as a Para - military instructor, in training university students in disciplinary matters, foot drills and physical fitness exercises. This was the student's initial preparation in their training. Training approximately four hundred trails - blazers from all walks of life – male and female in getting involved in cotton picking, workshops, various skills and preparing them to enter the work force. I was still considered a member of the police force and promoted to a higher rank of a sergeant, with an increase in salary and benefits.

The developing National Service camp was located in Kimbia in the interior location and not too far from the Jim Jones's camp. No one knew of the existence of such camp and its activities that were taking place in that area of Kituma. There were rumors and speculations, that those acres of land in the interior were sold by the government to Pastor Jim Jones and his contingent of criminal Hench men, who were armed with guns and other weapons. The outcome was that eight hundred souls were murdered including a Congressman Ryan from the United States of America, who was on a fact finding mission on reports of abused women and children in that camp.

I stay on with the National Service for over ten months and given a rent free house to live in. It was separated from the camp site, along with a plot of land, in doing my own farming in green vegetables. All training staff had spent time doing special training at other locations before entering Kimbia which was the main National Service camp. Vampire bats were rampant at nights in the jungle area. Every night one of our staff's and also a friend of mine big toe were being bitten by a vampire bat. Lots of blood was visible on his sheet on the bed when he gets up in the mornings. We all feared that our turn will be next; so we were vigilant on the lookout, in catching the vampire bat. It so happened, that in the hours of darkness, the bat flew in and heading straight for his victim's bed. The vampire bat then was attempting in getting under the sheet when a couple of us pounced on it – beating it with sticks until dead. The size of the vampire bat was a size of a rat - with its wing span at approximately eighteen inches across.

In the National Service main camp, pioneers picked cotton on the farm; and they were also involved in Para Military training along with the staff. I had organized boxing tournament on camp on the weekends - in having the youths letting out some of their steam in the boxing ring, rather than doing mischievous things on camp. At the end of the pioneers National Service training, a couple of the youths turned out to be good amateur boxing champions in the city.

On camp there was a certain big kid nick named "Baby Elephant." He was a staff trainee that frequently bullied many smaller pioneers in size on camp. I then confronted him about his bullying attitude. And he told me *"You can do what you want to do."* I then knocked him down and out with a left over hand punch, because he was taller than me. Since then, he never bullied anyone else, but he did show respect to everyone on camp.

Still being a police officer, I was vigilant and did not ignore or condoned any wrong doings on the camp site. However, it was reported that food stocks in the kitchen pantry were running low too often every the month. I suspected that one of the cooks was stealing the food items from the pantry, So, I left my residence at midnight, lying low out side the camp's perimeter fence, looking for any unusual activities at the back door of the kitchen. What I observed was that two strangers standing at the fence, while the cook was handing them food items in boxes in exchange for money. I sounded an alarm which caused them in scattering in various directions. The next day, the cook was dismissed off the camp - with arrangements being made for him to be transported by aircraft out into the city.

I and a contingent of the National Service staff were assigned in clearing bushes in-dept of a main highway. It was an idea of the government of the seventies in building a new highway in Guyana, and stretching all the way to our neighboring country Brazil. We worked in the summer when the sun was at ninety degrees hot - cutting tree stumps with pick axes. However, the work was permanently halted after a few months. Now in the new millennium, I was notified by someone that travelled from the USA to Guyana that the new government had finished building the highway – it is now running from Guyana to Brazil.

A Military Life

I left the National Service in joining the Guyana Defense Force as an officer cadet. The Training Corp's Cadets Academy started off with approximately sixty cadet officers; and at the end of the training only thirty five cadets graduated on the passing out parade that was a year later. A Presidential ceremonial inspection parade of the passing out cadets was to take place on the square. We all were standing in ranks on the square awaiting the President who was more than an hour late on his arrival. My green beret that I had on was a little too tight on my head – it causing me to feel faint while standing at ease in over a ninety degrees sun. I felt nauseous and vomited, but I held it in - swallowing it back into my stomach in avoiding embarrassment to my fellow officer cadets; and in the presence of over a thousand spectators.

During cadet training, a certain cadet officer was disturbing half of the cadets in the barracks with his loud snoring and almost every night. So, we decided to catch a large beetle that carried two large frightening tentacles. One Friday night when he had started his loud snoring, we placed the beetle in his under wear. Immediately, the cadet sprung up from his bunk bed screaming aloud. Since after that episode, the cadet officer ceased snoring at night; and from there on the other cadets enjoyed a full night's rest.

On completion of my training, I was made principal instructor at the military academy for cadet officers. This training lasted another one year and with me doing the same training all over again, along with the new cadet officers. Jungle training was one of three requirements in training the cadet officers, in order in graduating from the academy. One night in the jungle, we took our ponchos and were setting them up as tents in resting up until the next day break. The cadets didn't do a proper sweeping of the camp; and someone did not follow the rules in burying the left over food at some distance away from the camp site. On retiring to bed I felt something wiggling under my back and under the ponchos. Immediately, I shouted *snake*: Causing the four of us scrambling out of the tent. In returning to the camp site armed with a flashlight, I saw a black snake at approximately four feet in length – it was instantly killed on the spot.

In jungle training, a cadet officer was given a bayonet, matches and a small amount of ration in lasting him for a few days in the jungle - its either you find a creek or you have to find the right vine for drinking water in order to survive. Officer Cadets in my time were cross trained into doing prison duties with the inmates, in the main prison in the city and at other Governmental institution, in case of a general strike at those facilities.

Later, I represented the Guyana Defense Force in the country annual pistol shooting championship on the pistol range. I trained very hard at the pistol range on a daily basis, before taking part in the competition. I was then crowned the champion in a running and deliberate shooting competition in that year. Subsequently, I was sent overseas, along with a contingent of two other officers and a platoon of men in participating in training with the Black Watch Special Forces in England. And they were considered to be the Scottish Guards. There, I took part in a running and shooting competition - challenging *a* team from that Special Forces. I came in second place, but I was told that I missed the bulls - eye by one shot. One of the Black Watch competitors had won the competition. However, I felt confident that I had shot all my bulls – eye.

Every day meals in the officer's Mess Hall in England were boring. It was steak, potatoes and tomatoes on a daily basis. So, I purchased junk food from the stores in and around the neighborhood close to the Heathrow Airport, where the officer's barracks and club was located.

As I was enjoying a program on television in the officer's barracks, one of the Black Watch officers came and told me to switch my channel, in viewing what was taking place in my country of Guyana. On doing so, I saw the entire scenario of the Jim Jones episode as I mentioned earlier. My platoon that I had left back home in Guyana was the first responders arriving at Kituma – the location where the killing had taken place. When we were leaving England and returning to Guyana on a British Airway jet plane; one of its engines caught fire. The pilot turned around the plane and headed back to the Heathrow airport in England; but first he dumped fuel from the left engine of the plane and into the ocean. The contingent of Guyanese soldiers later arrived safely, and we boarded another military plane that flew us to our national airport in Guyana.

An Impossible Task

Most officers that are attached to a battalion have to spend time at the border location for at least three months, which was far away from their homes. The low ranking soldiers and non commission officers spent a longer time. At times, soldiers get home sicknesses and they will do anything possible, so as to leave the camp site for home. Under a previous commander a soldier was excused off camp twice, because he reported that both his grandmother had passed away in his hometown and away from the location. When I relieved the present commanding officer at the location, the soldier later approached me, reporting that he needed to leave camp, because his grandmother had passed away; and that he wanted to attend her funeral. I was notified by the sergeant, that he had already left camp on two other occasions to bury his grandmothers. I did not grant him a pass this time around in burying his third grandmother. A week later, the said soldier mounted a machine gun, at approximately one hundred yards on high ground away from the camp and firing live ammo round on the camp site. Luckily no one was shot, but he was hunted down and arrested. The soldier was escorted back to the city and given a dishonorable discharge from the military.

In the1980's, the President of Guyana Forbes Burnham instructed the Guyana Defense Force commander in clearing a site, which was not far from the main airport. Soldiers were used as the main labor force, along with a captain under their command in completing the task in one month. The work was halfway finished and with only two weeks before the President breaking - ground ceremony was to take place at the new site. Panic erupted among the higher ranks in the Guyana Defense Force, in getting the task completed on time. So, they selected me and relieving the captain in charged at the job site. On visiting the work site, I knew that it was impossible in finish clearing that area, and also running electricity from the main street at four hundred yards into the area. The tree stumps were still remaining to be uprooted by soldiers with their pick axes. I said to myself "Why me as a junior officer rather than the captain, they should relief from that task?" So, the only thing left for me in doing was to pray to the Almighty God, in doing the impossible task - because, in the eyes of man, it was not possible in accomplishing that huge task. So, I went into a closet, falling on my knees, praying and sweating at the same time for over an hour. On completion of my supplication to God, I felt relieved, even before the task was actually completed.

In returning to the site the following Monday morning, I made a couple of requests to my senior commanding officer - requesting a bull dozer and an extra platoon of men, so that the task can be completed on time, in the President's visit and for the breaking ground ceremony. The work was done, with three days more to spare. Pre - visits by senior officer were made at the site and they were pleased with the work accomplished by me and the two platoons of men. The day of the ceremony, we were given praises by a few speakers, and finally by the President of Guyana himself. But I gave thanks to my God, to bailing me out of that impossible task. You can empower yourself with positive thinking and faith in the Almighty God.

Murder of a Soldier

As a former police officer, I was called to the Guyana Defense Force Headquarters and given a mission, in going back into the interior location in Lethem Rupunnuni, to investigating a missing soldier at the border camp location. On arrival at the military camp site, I hired an interpreter that spoke Portuguese and the English languages. Information received from the sergeant at the location that a private was missing over the weekend. The sergeant suspected that the soldier had crossed over the border into neighboring Brazil. The soldier crossed the border when the Irving River was low at ankle high, and taking a bottle of rum with him. His intensions were to get the natives in a drunken state in attempting to go to bed with one of their wives. It so happened that he succeeded, (i.e. after the woman's husband was stoned drunk; but the father- in –law was sober and he caught the soldier in the act of committing adultery with his daughter – in – law). The man took a machete, chopping the soldier to pieces and placing him in a bag and disposing the body parts in the Irving River, so that the alligators will feast on it.

During my investigation, I found the soldier's left side military booth and a bloodied machete abandoned on an empty fruit stand on the dam. The man's wife whom the soldier had slept with was sitting and washing clothes by the riverside on the Brazil side of the border. When I approached her, she refused in turning around when asked by the interpreter in doing so. I observed that one of her eyes was swollen to the extent of being tightly shut. I did not attempt further in questioning her about the swollen eye. I came to the conclusion that her husband had assaulted her. I later took my written report to the Brazilian Federals, in them to take action by arresting the father – in – law for the murder of the Guyanese soldier. They however concluded that the action taken by the father – in - law was lawful. Through my interpreter, I was told that if a man is caught in bed with another man's wife – whosoever finds him in the act can kill him – that was the end of my investigation.

I was later given another task from the Headquarters of the GDF, in monitoring a Canadian oil company that was drilling for oil in the Ruppununi district. Subsequently, I received word from the top brasses that the drilling had been cancelled. This was due to an on going dispute with our government and the oil company. However, what I later learned is that the oil company wanted to divide the profit unfairly - in taking fifty one percent to forty nine percent in their favor. My task was in ensuring that the company had stopped all operation in drilling for crude oil. In 2013, I was informed that the new government in Guyana had come to an agreement with the Canadian Oil Company, in splitting the profit far less than forty nine percent in favor of the Canadian Oil Company.

Previously, the information that I received from a Brazilian citizen – is that the government of Brazil was furious and dissatisfied with our government about the matter of drilling for oil during an ongoing dispute of land between the two countries – but it may have been a rumor.

During my stay in the Ruppununi, a Guyana Defense Force helicopter pilot: One of my squad mate was assigned, in flying me around on a daily basis in checking on the Canadian oil company, and ensuring that no drilling was taking place on the land. While returning back to base camp we spotted a huge deer wandering in the savannah. We began chasing the deer whilst flying at a low altitude and at tree top level. The deer had us flying in circles for about five minutes, because it was turning around in the opposite direction every time we tried getting lower to the ground. The deer soon became exhausted by the steady and non stopping chase. And flying at a low level, I took my service pistol – firing a shot directly to the center of the deer's body but missing it. I then fired my second shot after aiming at his nose, and hitting it in the region of the heart - it causing the deer to fall to the ground stone dead. We eventually touched down, picking up the deer which weighed approximately one hundred and fifty pounds and carrying huge anthills. The deer was taken back to the military camp and given to the cook who was shorting of fresh meat that was late on arriving from the headquarters. It was my first time eating delicious deer meat.

On my way home from the military camp, I observed black smoke coming out of my neighbor Thom's house. I realized that someone else other than an adult was in the house. When I looked under the steps, there was a small fire and lots of smoke. There was a little girl cuddled up in a corner and under the stairs, but she was not moving. Immediately, I picked her up and transported both kids to the hospital in my military jeep. The little girl's hair on her head was burnt to a char in the fire – she later died at the hospital.

Living in the USA

In 1984, I tendered my resignation with the military and I was given an honorable discharge, attaining the rank of first lieutenant. That is, after serving six years at a few Military locations. I then came to the United States of America with my family – my two daughters and a wife. I was planning in obtaining a GDL in driving an eighteen - wheeler Mack truck in going from state to state and avoid being in one place – but that plan did not work out to my advantage. My first civilian job in the USA was working as a security officer.

I had done CPR training on the job; and one day it came in useful to saving someone's life. That day, I was assigned to a security booth on the seventh floor, in the building where I was observing a few women and men running from the bathroom area. They were looking very perplexed and sad. I enquired what the matter was; and was told that a woman was laying on the floor and appearing to be dead. I then rushed over to the bathroom, in finding that the second in command of the security force was rendering CPR on the woman – by giving her compressions, but with no breaths. Lenny had enormous size hands that I had ever seen on a human being which can break anyone's rib cage. Immediately, I took over from the exhausted Lenny, started giving breaths and then compressions to the woman for about twenty five minutes, before she regained a pulse and breathe.

In the nineteen eighties, the response time of the EMS was twenty to twenty five minutes from the time that a call was placed to the emergency center. On arrival, the EMS representatives took over from me. Looking into the mirror, my eyes were blood – shot red from total exhaustion in rendering CPR to the female. The company awarded me with a letter of appreciation for saving the young woman's life. The said Asian young woman normally walked passes my station at the beginning of the day without saying good morning to any of the security officers. When she had recovered from her illness and from that day on she became friendly, in thanking me for saving her life. Ten months later I was promoted to a supervisor of security; responsible to all three buildings on the Broadway locations. In that year I was compensated with two bonuses- one in early February and the other in December 1986.

In 1987, I was asked to take a look at the fingerprinting system in the Human Resources Department, because they were in backlog, in submitting Prints to the Commodities Division and the Security Exchange Commission. The company had to pay thousands of dollars in penalties to the Commodities Exchange. I was given the opportunity in auditing the fingerprinting section in the Human Resources Department. And what I discovered was that instead of making two prints on the same day of hiring the employees. The staff only made one print of each person – that is, by sending them to the Commodities Exchange. It was very difficult for the fingerprinting expert in seeking out each and every branch of the company, in finding an individual, in re- taking a second fingerprint of that person. However, many of the brokers did not respond in a request for a second fingerprint to be taken from them. From there onwards, I was given the responsibilities of a newly created department - apart from the Human Resources Department. I was given the task in taking fingerprint of all new hires, drug testing, polygraph, urinalysis and doing a background test of most employees. Some executives were totally exempted from that process. I was subsequently promoted to a manager and given a hefty bonus at the end of the year.

In 1989, the Security Exchange Commission had started an investigation of the company for wrong doings, in junk bonds and their trading practices. The investigations that were done by the SEC had prolonged for over a year – even the FBI got involved in the investigations. At one point my office space was used in placing a microwave listening device, in picking up conversations throughout the day from certain executives working in their individual offices. The company finally caved in over a weekend discussions. This had involved the company's legal counselors and representatives from the SEC. That Monday morning most of the employees were given their walking papers. Some women were distraught, and they were shedding tears on their way out of the building.

Working at the company was a challenging experience, especially when the company was doing their monthly stocks and bond counts. I was responsible in having the combinations to the walk in vault, along with a deputy vice president of the company who alone had the key to the vault. We both had to be present at the same time in opening up the vault. And while on the floor observing the employees doing their counting, I saw from a distance on the floor, that an employee was slipping bond certificates into one of the garbage pails. On checking the garbage pail, I found a few bonds and stocks certificates worth millions of dollars intermingled among the garbage. The employee was immediately reported to the vice president in charge of the counting. From thereon and after the ending of each count, my department staff had to go through all the garbage pails, before the garbage were disposed of at the main garbage area in the rear of the building.

New procedures were now in place. The female employees had to replace their pocket books with company prescribed transparent plastic bags, before entering the counting area of work. After that incident, I had made constant rounds on checking the main garbage disposal site, which was located at the rear of the building as stated. What I witnessed was a non- employee sifting through the garbage. He was meticulously going through many of the print out sheets before putting them away in his briefcase. I approached closer to the area asking him to leave and he willing did so. Since then, a special water disposal company was rented by the company, in disposing all confidential printout and other confidential documents. The disposal was done by a process of shredding all documents to a pulp with water.

At the end of the fiscal year in the month of July, I was nominated employee of the year, among ten thousand employees in twenty five states in the USA; including satellite offices in Canada, Russia and England. For background checks in England was done differently from the other countries. If a company or other businesses are requesting a background check on an individual in England. In the eighties, they were granted permission, in checking through the newspapers in the archived section of the police station for any felonies committed by that person.

Working in the brokerage firm was very challenging, and it was a brand new experience to me. In the company they were no thirteenth floor in the building. All the executives had offices on the twelfth floor with an express elevator assigned in taking them up to their floor - and visa - versa. The bathrooms on the twelfth were situated differently from those that were on the rest of floors. The women's bathroom was on the right and the men's bathroom was on the left. I went blindly into the bathroom without looking at the signs and thinking that it was the men's room that I was entering. While sitting in the stall, I heard women high heels footsteps entering the bathroom. On looking through the crack in the door – it was only women seen gossiping in the bathroom. Immediately, I turned off my Walkie – Talkie radio in not alerting them that a male was intruding in an unauthorized space - when they should not have. So, when the coast was clear, I slipped out of the area unnoticed.

Executives had many privileges in the company. A dining room was situated on the top floor of the building. Toilet paper rolls in the bathrooms were adorned with colorful flower designs and it was thicker than the regular toilet paper - that idea caused me to start using napkins, instead of toilet paper. One has to fold the toilet tissue paper more than once before use. It was a money waster, in buying a thin roll of toilet tissue and having to fold it four times before using it.

A trusted employee is expected to be honest at all times on the job. Even when an infraction is being committed by that family member or friends in his presence or it has been reported to him by someone else in the work place. An employee is expected in reporting anyone committing an infraction in the work place. Security officers of the company were entrusted, in keeping order and protecting life and property. A Security Officer, who was working on the midnight shift, frequents himself on the top floor in the executive dining room. He was stealing the frozen ice cream every night during his tour of duty. The staff working in the dining room then notified me that they were shorting ice cream for the executives during lunch time. So, I later installed a candid camera in the dining room, in the act of catching him red handedly. The following day when reviewing the tape of the camera, I recognized the security officer that was suspected stealing the ice cream. It was obvious, because he was gaining weight rapidly on the job.

Many other complaints were forwarded to my department reporting, that the maintenance department was not honoring their requests, in relocating furniture or computers to their new offices. At times, the employees will have to be waiting more than a week before anything getting done. One weekend, I installed a candid camera in the maintenance office in finding out what activities was going on in that office, and what was causing so many delays, in responding rapidly to a request. A camera was activated in the maintenance office for one week. On reviewing the tape it was discovered that the supervisor, along with his entire crew was gambling for money while on the job. This incident was brought to the attention of the company board members; and the entire maintenance department was given their walking papers; and with a contracted maintenance company taking their place.

What I observed working at a Brokerage House in the city is that, it was very difficult for my department, in having brokers participating in fire drills. The excuses that the brokers will gave was *"We are on the telephone with our clients, negotiating a big deal with million of dollars, and we cannot leave our desk for just a stupid drill."* One mid - morning at the main office on Broad Street, a major fire broke out on the eleventh floor in the building. Many brokers were trapped on the floor, because of the thick black smoke that saturated the entire floor, and blinding their eyes from getting to the exit doors.

The chief of security and me proceeded to the area, in finding that a couple of male brokers had climbed through a window, and they were standing on a narrow ledge under the window. Eventually, we rendered some assistance in getting them unto a lower floor in the building. The security chief suffered smoke inhalation and he had to be treated by the EMS personnel's. And after that occurrence, an executive order was passed down to all vice presidents on the trading floor that it was mandatory for all traders to participate in fire drills.

A Strong Will

Another dishonest act had taken place – this time by a contract guard hired in working the night shift in another building and across from the headquarters. The security guard had abused the company's telephone in calling the 900 number, having sexual conversations with the girls on a nightly basis and during his tour of duty. In investigating the matter and going through all bills sent by the telephone company. That is, from day one that the officer was on board. To our astonishment, the bill amounted to twenty four thousand dollars. I then recommended that the security company's contract be voided – and for my company in contracting a more reputable security company, in taking their place. Management did so without any questions in accepting my recommendations.

A continuing dishonest act was committed by an in -house security guard who was with the company for many years. A quantity of gold was sent by American Express from an employee in California, and to be delivered to an executive of the company who was based in the New York office. The security guard had signed receiving the package, but he never did hand it over to the person the package was destined for. I had later done an investigation of the missing package in using the American Express tracking system. It was revealed, that the package was signed for by the said security guard working on the floor of the intended recipient. The gold was worth thousands of dollars. It was never recovered from the Guard, and the guard was never fired by management.

The first dramatic experience that I had witnessed on the job was a case of homicide. The murder had taken place in one of our buildings on Broadway in Manhattan. During the eighties, the bathroom doors were not properly secured, in term of having the appropriate locks on the doors. Around ten o'clock in the morning on the seventh floor, in another building across the street from the headquarters, when the vice president entered the men's bathroom. He was immediately followed close behind by an intruder into the bathroom. On reporting to the crime scene, the vice president body was later discovered lying on the floor in the bathroom in a pool of blood, appearing to be dead. It seemed that the VP was robbed and murdered by some unknown assailant who was trespassing on the seventh floor. Since after that deathly occurrence, I had installed combination locks on all bathroom doors in all our buildings downtown Manhattan.

A classic incident concerning a person disguised as an employee well – mannered, dressed in a suit and tie entering a trading floor one early morning. He first greeted the receptionist at the front desk. She was greeted with a friendly good morning, along with a smiling face. The intruder then proceeded to the back cubicles and out of sight of the receptionist's view. And then, he rampaged through all drawers in the employees cubicles, steeling monies with other valuables. The man then left by way of the emergency exit door leading out to the street. When the traders reported to work an hour later, they discovered that their cubicle spaces were violated along with many items stolen, including their identification access cards.

We all are born with the will in doing the things that we would like doing, or the thing we choose not to do: The will to creep and to walk; the will in scaling a high wall when we are chased by vicious dogs; and a will in kicking a habit.

When I was working at the Brokerage House, I had developed a habit of drinking before having dinner. At the end of the year, other company managers usually sent Christmas gifts in packages of either whisky or expensive wines. So, I found myself tempted in drinking the free liquor, prior having dinner. However, I decided that it was not the right thing I was doing; so I cleared all the whisky and wine bottles from the cabinet and emptying them in the kitchen sink. Sometimes, it will take something dreadful in happening to a person, before resolving a drug or drinking habits. However, I knew someone falling into a red ant nest and being bitten, before kicking a habit of drinking- a non — traditional or unconventional way in getting over an addiction.

The Security Industry

After leaving the brokerage house in Wall Street, I was later employed at a security company as a personnel manager, in conducting training classes in all security matters. I was also trained as a CPR and First Aid Instructor at the American Red Cross. And I have certified many staff at other programs free of charge. One Saturday morning, I was conducting orientation. And prior at the beginning of classes, I usually do a roll call of all new hires in the classroom. I had in my possession a list of names, along with identification cards of all new employees attending that orientation classes. One gentleman's name did not match the face on an ID card, so I had requested some sort of identification from him. Instead, he immediately got out of his chair and ran out through the exit door into the street.

One of my responsibilities was checking on the status of all foreign students' visas that were working for the security company; and keeping proper records of their expiration dates. Also, in assisting them in extending their stay and working permit in the United States of America. However, prior to me being the manager of the security company; a guard was hired with someone else's social security card. The guard was working for the company in over five years without being discovered; that he was illegally employed in the company or he was illegally in the country. It so happened, that a woman had filed for child support from her husband who was a dead beat dad; and that social security card

72

came under the same social security number. The check that the guard was receiving was garnished - with a percentage of money coming out of the pay check on a biweekly basis.

The guard with the garnished check made a complaint to the president of the company who in turn requested that I should look into the matter. My investigations revealed that the guard was in possession of another person's social security card, and he was working under the pretence of that person for a very long period of time. Without notifying him that he can no longer work for the agency - the guard never did show up for work again in the agency.

I was at my desk interviewing an eccentric looking man for a job in security. The individual had a thick side burns, reddish eyes and the teeth in his mouth were all pointed. He requested to be working at one of our warehouse at an industrial site. However, I did not hire him, because his documents were not in order, and he was not qualified for the position.

Community Organizer

My next place of employment was working at a non - profit organization as director of Plant Management, Security and Transportation for over twelve years.

And during my tenure at the Agency, I was appointed liaison officer to a precinct - having to attend monthly meetings. I was twice awarded for my involvement in community work, organizing parades, involving vendors, people in the community, Fire Department and the Police Department. The logo on the parades was, *"No drugs in my neighborhood."* The message was not well received by drug the dealers. But without any sort of resistance, they eventually moved their operation out of the neighborhood and into other areas.

Also, I have attended Auricular Acupuncture training classes at the Lincoln Hospital, under the supervision of a professional Acupuncturist. I am certified in administering acupuncture on persons for various addictions: Obesity; smoking; drugs and sleeping disorder, etc. I was involved in coaching the basket ball players in my organization in fitness training. And I was a recipient of a plaque, in my all out efforts in producing a fit team that was participating in many tournaments with other non profit organizations.

My time was also dedicated to a Head Start school program in the Bronx community. I had written an emergency response manual for a natural disasters and the releasing of a chemical or biological bomb in the air, in the vicinity of the school. All board members gave their approval to the written manual that I had submitted to the principle of the school. I was awarded with tickets for five people, in going on a boat ride on the *Spirit Cruise* around the island of Manhattan, in the city of New York; up the Hudson River and the East River.

The September 11th 2001 attack on the twin towers in New York City had caused me to lose focus at home, when I was hurriedly getting dressed in reporting to work in the Bronx. I had just finished cleaning my ears, but thoughtlessly forgetting a Q-Tip in my left ear. Then, I pulled my T- shirt over my head, when suddenly I heard a popping sound in my left ear. It was my ear drum that was ruptured and causing that sound. My left ear immediately started oozing blood.

Working at a drug program with clients that are abusive to drugs was not like taking a stroll in the park. It was very challenging - and you had to be gutsy.

Earlier, working on the job, I was not welcomed with open arms by most of the clients. And prior to me working there, the clients were in control – in working a system to their own advantage and benefit. Clients will pay five dollars or more in having someone standing in a line in the street, in holding a position for them. That is, before arriving later in the morning, at the opening up of the clinic for the dispensation of their meditation. In attempting in putting a stop to their schemes, I was threatened to be shot or capped in the knee if I shut down their scheme. However, I eventually restored order in the clinic; and gradually, they showed me some sort of respect.

A few years working with the agency, I converted a storage basement into an activity center for both the clients and staff, in relieving their stress. I named that facility **"Stress less"** The newly renovated basement was used for games, meetings and other functions by all, including outsiders of the Agency; especially for Christmas parties given by other agencies. Working at my Agency, I had on many instances in displaying the ability to solving problems which benefitted the entire Agency. I had used the latest technology in catching two staff members, in the act of stealing their fellow workers checks or monies. This usually had taken place when the staff was at meetings and away from their offices.

Another dishonest act had involved a counselor and a female client who was very desperate, in getting back her children from the City Agency. The counselor took the advantage of his position, in demanding cash payment from the client, before making it possible for the client in getting back her kids. I had set up a sting operation with the client, in catching the counselor, in the act of receiving the money that I had saturated with red invisible dye. The day when the counselor had taken the monies – the dye got all over his hands. When the counselor began sweating, and he began wiping his face with his hand, the dye got on his face - it making him resembling a circus clown.

My next job was working as a Real Estate agent – buying and selling properties in New York City. In 2007, the economy went sour and the housing industry became fallible. I was discouraged and was no longer interested in the Real Estate business.

One of the many reasons in leaving the Real Estate business was - I had witnessed other brokers and agents not being honest in dealing with their clients. Some of the agents were displaying an unprofessional and unethical behavior during the process of buying or selling properties.

Some sleep not except they have done mischief and evil, in causing some to fall.

Visions, Prophesies and Prodigies

*T*hroughout my adult life my heavenly father has definitely gotten my attention in many ways. He has indicated to me on many occasions - either by a vision, dream or He presented things that are genuinely real; and that He is in control of everything on planet earth. God has shown me that nothing is impossible for him in accomplishing. And I should not doubt Him, but have faith in Him in performing these miracles.

"Can a scientist explain in simple language, what is the difference between a miracle and magic?" I had a unique experience in Jerusalem in the Treasured Land. This took place while visiting the Wailing Wall. There are two halves at the wall – the male goes to the left and females to the right. In 2005, prayer requests were written down on a piece of paper and then stuffed in a crack of the wall. At the entrance to the square where all are gathered in prayers at the wall, a heavy set male, donned in a shawl from head to toe began prophesying at the entrance. He caught my attention, because of his boisterous message in the Hebrew language. When the man had finished his message, he walked through the crowded square; approaching me face to face and asking me in a perplex manner *"Who are you?"* I then told him where I was born and why I was visiting Jerusalem.

After taking the man's photograph with my camera and developing it on my return to the USA. There was no head seen, but only the clothes were visible in the film.

Beginning in the year 2001, my entire life has since been changed from a worldly one to a spiritual life. It feels to me that I am at times looking down from above and witnessing the disasters taking place in our tiny world. Even though, the visions that I receive places my human body at locations on planet earth. It is very depressing at times when awakening from having these visions from God; and there is nothing that I can do, in preventing those cycles or natural or predestined disasters destined for our planet. Some of the episodes I am relating in this memoir are experiences actually had taken place.

Early in the morning on Tuesday September 11th 2001, I had a vision that appeared very real to me. It placed my spirit in one of two towers at the World Trade Center in Manhattan New York. My spirit was positioned in a way, that the first thing I saw was a large engine stuck in a corner and way up in the ceiling on the floor. Then, I found myself looking through a window panel, viewing nothing but black and white stuff floating in the air. Primarily, what immediately came to my mind was the Hudson River overflowing. Prior to that vision, I had a premonition that I should take a vacation - even though I did not plan in going anywhere special, but only staying at home. Normally the route I take in getting to work on a daily basis was driving over the Manhattan Bridge, via Manhattan to the Bronx.

The morning of September 11th 2001 at approximately 8:45am, I received a landline phone call from my ex - girl friend - her telling me to turn on the television. On doing just that, I saw one of the twin towers on fire. Minutes later, I witnessed what appeared to be a small plane approaching the towers. And as it was getting closer, I realized that it was a larger plane about to crash into the second tower - it did so. The impact had displayed a huge fireball at the corner of the building. Both towers looked like two large chimneys with their flue gushing out the black smoke high into the air. I then took out my video camera and started recording the fiery scene in Downtown Manhattan, on Fox News channel five station; by switching back and forth to CNN, where some of the actions were more amplifying. I cut short my vacation time in returning to work, because I played a key role on my job as Chief of Security, Plant Management and Transportation.

In the Bronx neighborhood, people printed the burning twin towers on tea shirts and were selling them for ten dollars a pop - I then purchased one. On taking it home and washing it. To my astonishment, the entire tea shirt was taken over with black mold. It was insanitary in wearing the tea shirt - it was one of the weirdest things that I had ever witnessed.

October 2001, I saw in a vision that a security person in New York City was pushing back another attack in the underground sewer. What appeared in my vision was someone attempting in penetrating the city of Manhattan, but he was unable to. And so far the terrorists are unable, in carrying out a successful attack in the city. In the year 2002, I experienced an earthquake happening close to the Canadian border. In my vision and what I saw were high mountains crumbling in a wavelike fashion in the United States of America. This vision was given to me when I had decided in migrating permanently to Canada. However, I had a change of heart after that vision. So far that vision has not yet come to pass. In 2003, I received advice from above in a vision while I was sleeping, that I needed *spiritual guidance*. A large banner was displayed, accompanied by a loud voice – and the words were written in large bold letters "**SPIRITUAL GUIDANCE.**"

On May 19th 2004, I had a wonderful vision that I was standing in a huge mansion. It was in an open area with no one in sight. Suddenly, but adjacent to me I saw my ex- wife appearing, then immediately disappearing out of sight. Instantly, a pale face woman, approximately five feet eleven inches appeared in front of me. Her hair was shoulder length. I then found myself in the kneeling position and with my left hand outstretched - even without her giving me any instructions in doing that. The woman appeared to be in her forties according to our Gregorian calendar. She then slipped an *insignia ring* on to my middle finger on my left hand – it was a perfect fit. And she never instructed me to stand up, but I found myself standing in the upright position. The woman said these words to me in the English language. "*Your name is now Roundtree, and Roundtree is the richest ever... wherever you go you will be recognized*". Then she immediately appeared behind my female friend who was standing twenty feet to my right. The woman's behavior towards her was not a pleasant one. She hastily tore out something in and around the region of the woman's back, telling her in a low tone of voice that ***"Your name is Roundtree"***. And without seeing her walking in my direction, she suddenly appeared in front, escorting me to a large room that carried no door, but only a passage way.

That female working in concert with the Creator was medium built, but attractive looking. She was very business like and officious in carrying out her routines. She accompanied me to the entrance of a large room, but stopped short in entering and immediately disappeared from my view. Another image suddenly appeared in the far corner of the room. I saw the back of a single chair in the far corner of the room - it was while I was standing at approximately twenty feet away. The chair suddenly was suspended in the air at approximately eighteen inches off the floor. Then, it suddenly began turning around in a clockwise manner and slowly facing in my direction.

Sitting in the chair was a male; also with a pale face and approximately five feet in height. My measurement assessment was based on the size of the chair the image of a man was sitting in. His hair was white as snow and covering his forehead with a bang – just like the Romans with a Julia Caesar style. He was donned in a pure white shawl from his shoulder down to his feet. He gave me a very friendly, but a penetrating and pleasant smile, which made me instantaneously joyful by his awesome and humbleness. The radiation of that smile stayed within me to this day. In waking up from that vision, I had attempted in figuring out His age, but to no avail. He appeared to be under a hundred years old and at the same time over a hundred. Meeting the Creator of the heavens and the earth was a great honor and everlasting experience. Even though it is said that ***one cannot see God and live***. But seeing him in spirit – it is not the case. *Others in the Old Testament have seen God face to face, and they lived to talk about it.*

Due to a dream that my ex - girl friend had about donating funds to a synagogue. I later visited a synagogue in the Queens County in the year 2005. I met a very humble and friendly woman who greeted me at the door. She was the sister of a Rabbi of the synagogue that is located below her apartment – her name is Deborah. I told her that I was seeking a synagogue to worship in and at the same time learn to speak the Hebrew language. She immediately volunteered in taking me on a tour in and around the synagogue. What I saw was not very encouraging, after comparing it with churches that I worshipped in. And in no way, it came close in terms of comfort and to fellowship in. However, Deborah invited me back to fellowship in the synagogue - and I did so reluctantly. A couple of months went by and the members were struggling, in coming up with donations for the rehabilitation of the synagogue. I volunteered in contributing funds in buying the materials and giving free labor for the enhancement of the synagogue. It took about two months, in completing all the renovation and enhancements of the synagogue. The total bill amounted to sixty four thousand dollars in labor and materials - in which I footed the entire payment for the contractor and materials.

The Rabbi and his congregation were very much satisfied with the final outcome of the work done within the synagogue. I was presented with a gift and a well written letter of appreciation from the Rabbi himself.

In 2005, Deborah requested that I gave a speech on the anniversary of her father's death. Her father was the Rabbi and the original founder of the synagogue. I had prepared a written speech and delivered that speech on February 18th 2005 - it was well received by the congregation and its members. And the following year, I was again asked to do another speech on the anniversary of Deborah's father. Behold, I got a message in a dream from my biological father who had passed away over forty years ago. He told me not to deliver that speech, which I had prepared in writing. However, I did decline from giving that speech on that occasion. In the said year, I had a vision that placed me on top of a mountain ridge in Israel. I was standing next to a tall figure who was wearing a white shawl covering the head and down to the feet. That person was looking straight ahead and whispered to me saying that ***"July 15th 2007, tragedy shall come to this land."***

What I saw were many people standing below a mountain ridge. They were a mixed crowd of men, women and children. Some of the children were in the arms of their parents and they were shedding tears. The site at the scene was melancholy and totally depressing. It was twilight time with the sun going down in the west. The sound of weeping and moaning was coming from the people gathered down below the mountain ridge. Later, I was determined in finding that mountain ridge where I stood in the Treasured land. So, I registered and booked for a church tour group bound for Israel.

On arriving in Israel a special driver by the name of David Ben Hur was assigned, in taking me around at the various tour sites in Israel, because I had been detached from the tour group after arriving at the air port in Tele – Aviv - or it had appeared to be the case. I found myself alone with the driver in all the tours I was on, including a boat ride in the Sea of Galilee. I visited the famous wall in Jerusalem, which tourists and residents of Israel visited on a regular basis - either to pray or sticking a prayer request in the crack or crevice in the wall. I later learned that no longer, piece of paper are allowed to be forced into the cracks on the wall.

Before arriving in Israel, I had pre planned in giving a reasonable donation to any Ethiopian Jewish Organization that is based in Jerusalem. I made a few phone calls, and finally making contact with someone that identified himself as an elder. He later came to my hotel room on the seventh floor, accompanied by two other men all dressed in white gowns. We then spoke for a while, and I handed him five hundred US dollars in cash donations. The monies had supposed to be going towards his organization. But they seemed very disappointed with the sum of money they had received, when they were leaving my hotel room. Early next morning, I had a very disturbing and uncomfortable dream. The message in the dream was that I had made a terrible mistake, in thinking that the monies given to the men were definitely not the true receivers of that donation.

In returning to the USA, I went to a Rabbi at another synagogue, rather than my regular synagogue. I told him about the vision I had, and what was told to me by the unidentified person in my dream, who notified me about what will befall the people in the land of Israel. He said that he does not believe in dreams, but he recommended me seeing a fellow Rabbi at another synagogue. The Rabbi at the other synagogue suggested, that I should go to the Israeli Consulate and report what I saw in my vision.

In the Month of April 6th 2006 while in a dream at night, I heard a clear voice saying, *"You are a descendant of a King,"* and nothing else did I hear in that dream. In April 29th 2006, something strange took place at my home in the presence of three other eyewitnesses - it was on a Friday at the beginning of Sabbath. Two candles were lit on the Sabbath table - it was a Jewish custom to bringing in a new day that starts at sundown. The candles went out instantaneously without a wind being present. All windows and doors were closed, and there was not a presence of a ceiling fan. My girl friend started speaking in English, as if she was prophesying a message. She was saying, *"Son - do trust in me and but only me"*. Sitting at the table in the usual manner and position, we were caught unaware with that strange voice coming from her. It was not her own voice; and I did not receive the full message from the beginning of her prophesy. On completion, she had appeared to be disoriented. She then had to be comforted at the table momentarily. My ex girl friend has acquired that gift from God, in prophesying certain things that are always coming to pass.

In the year 2007, a war between Hezbollah and Israel took place on July 15th 2007 as I was told by an unidentified person in my Dream in the year 2005. March 2007, I heard a voice telling me in my dream that *"If you become a Jew, you would* have *to change your name... the name that was given to you by God"*. In that dream, I insisted that my name cannot be changed under any circumstances. In looking around, I saw a tall and very thin Ethiopian man standing ten feet away from me. He did not identify himself as an Ethiopian man, but somehow I knew in my vision that he was Ethiopian. A few months later in the said year, the same Ethiopian man again came in my dream, and he repeated the same message to me.

On April 4th, and the 9th 2007, I saw in my vision while asleep at night that fire was falling from the skies – in February 15th, 2013 an actual meteorite exploded over Russia, and injuring over 1,100 people. May 2007 I had a vision that I was among several men singing along with them a beautiful song of Jerusalem. I woke up finding myself

singing that wonderful song. On Monday, August 13ᵗʰ 2007 I dreamt
that a tall building in the city of Manhattan was set on fire. A voice told
me that the building had contained asbestos. So, the next day I gave
my girl friend a mask to take to her workplace in case that my dream
comes to past. On Saturday, August 18ᵗʰ 2007, five days after my dream,
I heard on the news that a high rise building containing asbestos was
ablaze, and two fire fighters had lost their live. December 22ⁿᵈ 2007 I
dreamt that I was elevated in a chair with other men. I distinctly heard
a clear voice saying over and over again, ***"Jesus Christ is the son of
God"***- but I paid no attention to the voice. *I further state that I was not
a believer in Christ as the son of God - and that he did not arose from the
dead and ascending up to heaven.*

Saturday June 21ˢᵗ 2008, in a dream, I heard a man's voice describing
himself as the **Prophet Samuel**. I heard the voice saying, *"**I have a
message from God**"*. He said, not in such loud tone of a voice. ***"Speak
to me at Samuel 22."*** The next morning, I checked the scripture on *2
Samuel 22* that spoke about King David the one that God loved very
much. Previously, I was enquiring from God: Why was He giving me
all these visions and dreams – and who am I? I n the same year 2008,
I had a vision that there would be an attack on the day of *Rosh Kodesh*,
but I did not know or could identify the location. My spirit was in
an unknown area where soldiers were in their barracks and relaxing
with their guards down. In my spirit I warned them that the enemy
was surrounding the barracks - and they responded by fending off the
enemy.

It came to past, that in 2008 in a vision, I saw a woman in an
apartment praying over what appeared to be a cooked chicken or a
turkey. She wore a head scarf, and she was dressed in a long skirt or
a dress. I later learned that it was on a Thanksgiving holiday, along
with *Rosh Kodesh,* that the woman was ceremoniously celebrating. In
the vision, some men were dressed in black outfit and lying on their
stomach with guns in the ready position – it was along an embankment
close to water. As my spirit was walking along a narrow road, I saw
men maneuvering like soldiers, and they were in the ready position in
attacking. However, they were countered by the soldiers in Mumbai

India. *It was the said on the news that in the country where I saw was Mumbai India. A Rabbi and his wife, along with other Jews were killed by the terrorists.* In the said year, I dreamt that a truck had run over my mom's head. Two weeks later my mom was taken from the nursing home to the hospital with her face swollen, along with bruises on her cheeks. When I visited her and enquiring from the doctor the reason for her face being swollen with bruises. He told me, that they cannot diagnose what really happened to her, but he will continue in doing more tests.

January 3rd 2009 early morning hours between 5:30 am and 6:00 am I had a vision, that put me to an unknown house and in an unknown place. The house had a balcony overlooking the ocean. And I witnessed a huge tidal wave about a hundred feet in the air rolling towards me, while I was sitting in a chair on the balcony. But its water did not touch me. Soon after, a second wave came in doing the same. Later, I told my family and friend about the vision I had before; and it had actually took place on October 29th and 30th 2012. It came to past that on October 2012, New York and New Jersey was struck by a mother storm by the name of "*Sandy*" which caused enormous damage to those cities.

On the thirty eight day of the Omer count - which fell on Saturday May 16th 2009, I had another depressing vision pertaining to the city of New York. My spirit had wandered around a city, but observing that no one or vehicles were moving around the city. The city was devastated by what appeared to be a flood. Tall buildings were abandoned and the city looked derelict. My spirit surveyed the city from a vantage point by looking through a glass panel and assessing the damages. It was hurricane Sandy on October 29 2012. August 15th 2009 I had a vision that I was working on my book titled "**You are younger than your age.**" I had promised my regular barber who is Jewish, that I will show his Rabbi the new calendar of the world which I was working on. However, in my dream and while walking along a narrow road, I heard dogs barking behind me. In looking around, there were three vicious dogs grayest in color, but a man was controlling them on a leash. In my right peripheral vision, was what appeared to be a statue in the cemetery that looked like a person donned with a veil. And in front of me, and about two hundred yards was a monstrous snake like creature in the sea, with a portion of its trunk and head visible.

The next morning, I awoke up very depressed by the dream. So, I prayed fervently to my father in heaven for protection from my enemies that are seeking to cause me bodily harm. My prayers were answered in a dream on August 25th 2009, at approximately 3:33 am in the wee hour in the morning after retiring to bed. What I saw in my vision were three dogs closely behind me, but controlled by a man who had them on a leash. One dog broke loose and was charging towards me - followed by another close by. The dog in the lead sprang at my upper body and was attempting in getting to my throat; but I put my hands out, and he snatched on my hand, which immediately was covered by a thick padded- like material. I had two other dreams confirming, that Yahweh Himself came down from heaven to planet earth in flesh. Actually, He is one of the seven spirits standing on the right in front of the creator that ascended back to heaven. Prior to these dreams, I had another in November 2009.This was after I had doubted the Christians, that *Yehshua* is God Himself that came down to earth.

January 2010, I heard a voice distinctly saying in my dream, "***I was the son of God that came down to earth.***" Awakening the said morning, I felt ashamed of myself in doubting that Christ is God. Prior to the dream, I had made mockery of many Christians; even in arguing scriptures with my younger brother who is an ordained Bishop in the Christian Church. January 1st and 13th of 2010 I had a very clear vision of many shiny objects in the sky crossing each other from east to west, along with numerous other things doing the same maneuvers. This vision has not yet come to pass.

February 26th 2010, I had a vision where I witnessed in steering through a window of a house. I saw the earth was slowly expanding, and something with a large head and many teeth coming out of a hole in the ground – it appeared to be a lion cub. Next, I saw a child, approximately two years old sitting among a beautiful bed of flowers around the edge of the hole. A couple of lads began chasing the cub, which suddenly turned into a full grown lion - then transforming into a man. Instantly, I found myself leaving the house and standing in a grocery store. The

lion that was transformed to a man said to me, *"I know who you are."*
February 28th 2010 I had a vision where I saw very dark clouds twirling
around in the sky and with a huge opening up like an eye. At 1:00 pm
on Thursday 15th July 2010, I went shopping at Costco Wholesale in
Five Town Long Island. I parked my car in the usually spot in the lot
whenever I go shopping. The sun was very hot, and the parking lot had
other parked car with no other person in sight.

From a distance of fifty feet away, I saw a youth approaching in my
direction. He was walking towards me a bit slower than the average
person. My first impression was, that he was about to ask me for money,
but he did not. He was thin, about five feet six inches tall and wearing
a black head dress with a lump on the top closer to the front of the
forehead. Without me uttering a word to him he said, *"You are a lucky
man"* In saying that he gestured in a circular manner with both hands
and saying at the same time *"You have something shining around
your head."* I asked him where is he from; and his reply was *"I am from
Punjab India"* He in turn asked me the same question and I told him
that I am from South America. He then turned about and walked in the
same direction in which he came – walking without faltering in a slow,
but unusual manner. When bending down, in picking up trash from
the passenger side of my car, and just for a second. Looking around the
parking lot, the youth was nowhere to be seen. He did not get into a
car, because he was too young to drive, and no other car was in motion
at that moment. I was astounded, and I started calling all my closest
friends telling them about my experience, that I had encountered in
the parking lot.

December 23rd and also on the 30th of 2011, I saw in a vision while
asleep in the wee hours in the morning, that portents and shiny things
were displaying in the skies by crossing each other from two directions.
My visions have not yet come to pass.

Some time in 2012, I ran into a Rabbi that I had known from one of
my synagogues that I attended. He greeted me in an enthusiastic manner
saying *"there is a light shining around your head.* And he continued,
*"I saw you in my dream and you were teaching me… I know who
you are."* In 2012, I went to Costco Wholesale to purchase Super B12

vitamin tablets. After checking the shelves, I was disappointed that they had run out of the vitamin. On returning to my car, I observed a large sealed bottle of the said vitamin sitting on a curb at the passenger side of my car when I was about to open the car trunk.

February 2012, I saw in a vision that a very dark cloud was rolling and then opening up in the sky. June 2012, prior to the results of the general election in November 2012, I saw in a vision while asleep in the night, that President Obama was taking a victory lap along the isle, celebrating his victory in the final Election count. And, I also heard a loud voice saying, 'Conservative." Present Obama did win the election. This vision was told to members of my boxing team. January 3rd 2013 in a vision while taking a nap in the afternoon, I saw that the sun was beaming down on to earth in an unusual way that caught my attention. In July 2013, there was heat wave in the USA, Japan and Europe. The temperatures reached some places at 129 degrees. July 22nd 2013, around 2:00 am in the morning, I saw in my vision that soldiers dressed in olive green uniforms and caps mustering on the Israeli border. That dream is still yet in coming to pass.

Birth and Death of Christ:

The birth and death of Christ falls in the first month on the 14th day on the Prophetic calendar. On the Gregorian calendar, some examples of Christ's birthday and His death will fall on the following dates:

October 30th 2012 (29th)
March 24th 2014 (23rd)
July 17th 2015 (16th)
November 9th 2016 (8th)
March 4th 2018 (3rd)
June 27th 2019 (26th)
October 20th 2020 (19th)

Behold, the Lord will come with fire and His Chariots like a whirlwind, to render His anger with fury and His rebuke with flames of fire. Isaiah 66:15

I was guided by the Holy Spirit into reading Ecclesiastes 12:12 that states: *And further by these my son, be advised of making many books. There is no end and much study is a weariness of the flesh.* (i.e. scholars, politicians, religious leaders, scientists and other professionals cannot solve the chaotic problems in the world. The Almighty God, the Creator of all things; and He who is the light of the world, can change all situations.

Summary

For the frequent visions that I am having and prior to them, there are no precognition either during the day or at night. And in the beginning of my childhood at the age of nine years old, I was very curious in knowing who the Christ was that the Catholic Church strictly honored. So, I began seeking him; and finally after all these years, he invited my spirit into His mansion so, that I can have a face to face with him – and in convincing me that He is real. I am not religious or am I affiliated with any religion. That visitation, in having a face to face with him, has made me change from my worldly pleasures to my spiritual awareness's - it is like changing my DNA.

It can be justifiable in saying that parents and teachers are responsible in what the children are reading in school and at home. Many kids in this generation are more into playing violent video games on the computer or other electronic equipment; rather than going unto the playing field, in getting involved with physical activities. Most parents are unaware, that their kids are frequenting the public library – not in reading proper books, but in playing violent games on the computer – it is like learning, and expressing themselves in becoming violent at a higher level.

For the present generation solely relies on electronic equipment, in doing their daily assignments or home work. Without the availability of such technology students are becoming helpless. Students should be able to maximize their human resources and energy when electronic devices malfunction or when they are not available. In the beginning of my youthful days until present, I have displayed a very good, and very bad examples in the eyes of my friends and family. But one of my good examples is that I have initiated a tangible amount of fresh ideas through a level of curiosity, in the face of many adversities in my life. But I did set my goals and objectives in determining the course of action that I would take – it has paid off well in my adult life.

I have identified my inner strengths, tapping into my hidden talents and capabilities that I have possessed over a period of years. The ultimate goal in my endeavors is getting over a message of change. And especially to the younger generation who can successfully achieve their fullest potentials, in exploiting their under utilized capabilities – only awaiting someone else in tapping into them. I have developed a passion over the years for boxing. I have a dream that some day I will be able in opening up my own boxing gym in New York City; and maybe later open others in states like California and Los Angeles. The older generation can be a role model and a mentor to the youths of today. The educators, police officers, parents and other professionals can reinforce or motivate the ambitious younger generation, in radiating their self confidence, by making themselves important in their communities. I am intelligent enough to have a common sense approach in every thing I have applied throughout my life.

"If you do not effectively market the value of yourself by showing self- worth and integrity- no one will support your views, or have a genuine interest in your concepts" Every human and humankind was created on planet earth for a purpose. And during the years, in living through this journey; and before the time in our lives expires; we have a substantial role to play on planet earth. I believe that through my stubbornness, and being a strong willed person with unshakeable faith with scruples and values. It has brought me closer to the Creator for the rest of my spiritual life, in which I chose to live.

For some babies are still born, deformed or handicap for a purpose, while others are destined in becoming professionals, and in all aspects in life. But on the flipside, there are the evil- doers operating in a negative capacity in society, on this large rotating stage that we deemed as planet earth. For the law enforcement officers are fundamentally justified in carrying out their duties, in maintaining law and order, in protecting the lives and property of their state because of these evil - doers. And the democratic nations are the ones through diplomacy are resolving the conflicts all over the globe, by protecting us from those tyrants and terrorists.

In today's public schools some contemporary students will have an advantage, in utilizing a calculator in the class room, in analyzing a mathematical problem. But in my teenage days there was no such technology, in applying to the class rooms. A student will not be sufficient or able in excelling in science or mathematic, if the teachers are permitting them, in maximizing the use of calculator. Students must be able in conditioning their minds so as to have a strong power of analytical reasoning, in solving mathematical problems.

Personally, I had to learn from the two time tables to eighteen time tables from Elementary to Secondary (High School). It assisted me in solving mathematical calculations with confidence, a good retention of time tables, accuracy and maximum efficiency – and with some time to spare in the examination room. The English language in my opinion is rapidly fading away from the younger generation. It is replaced by the lingo text that they are using in communicating to their peers. Some typical examples the youths are intercommunicating and interacting are absolutely questionable. They are as follow:

LML – Laughing mad loud
LMAO – Laughing my ass off
WYD – What you doing?
BRB – Be right back
K – Ok
BTW By the way
ILY – I love you
2nite – Tonight
JK – Just kidding
NP – No problem
TTYL – Talk to you later
OMG – Oh my God

The above listed lingo text are not intelligible to the older generation like myself. But it is very much stimulating and acceptable to the younger generation. For this type of lingo is not proficiently, effectively or is it strong vocabulary, in elevating a student in reading at a favorable or professional level.

Another issue is the online courtship that I think is not so helpful in any way or means; and in properly communicating fluently in comparison to meeting face – to - face with someone. This type of communication can be extremely dangerous, disastrous; or it may well work perfectly for some lucky individuals. But when you are able in seeing that person face to face, you can make a better evaluation of them. A relationship is like entering the darkness with not seeing anything until your eyes get well adjusted to the darkness. Then you will be able to see a little light that is intermingling in the darkness.

"God is covered with a thick dark cloud, but if you diligently seek Him you will see His shining light in that darkness"

As predicted in my first book ever titled "**You are younger than your age**"- the ending of a twenty one years cycle which will be December 17th 2013 on the Gregorian calendar; and the 15th of the twelfth month on the Prophetic calendar in the year 5510. However, my life has more episodes to come in the future after the publication of this memoire. Prophesies may be handed down to me; and with more intensified tribulations of natural disasters in this world.

I have attended Jersey State College in graduating in certification in Security Administration, and the New York Technical College in Building Engineer /Maintenance.

And finally, I can consider myself a utopian that is extremely versatile, in possessing a personal magnetism and visionary leadership abilities, in analytical thinking and at the same time being very zestful. Judge me not in my past acts and conduct, that I have displayed in my younger days and my adult life.